ISO 9001, The Standard Interpretation

The International Standard System for Assuring Product and Service Quality

Second edition, completely revised

by Leland R. Beaumont

ISO Easy, P.O. Box 21, Middletown, NJ 07748 U.S.A.

Electronic mail address: info@isoeasy.org

www.isoeasy.org

ISO 9001, The Standard Interpretation

The International Standard System

for Assuring Product and Service Quality

By Leland R. Beaumont

Published by:
ISO Easy
P.O. Box 21
Middletown, NJ   07748 U.S.A.
Electronic mail address: info@isoeasy.org
www.isoeasy.org
Phone: (732)-671-7130
Fax: (801)-340-4690

All rights reserved. No part of this publication may be reproduced in any form, in an electronic retrieval system or otherwise, without prior written permission from the publisher, except for the inclusion of brief quotations in a review. The text of the ISO 9001 Standard is reprinted with the permission of the American Society for Quality Control.

Copyright © 1995 by Leland R. Beaumont
Printed in the United States of America

Other books by this author, published by ISO Easy:
ISO 9001, The Standard Companion

Publisher's Cataloging in Publication Data
Beaumont, Leland R.
ISO 9001, the standard interpretation : The international standard system for assuring product and service quality / Leland R. Beaumont. — 2nd ed., completely revised
p. cm.
Includes index, bibliography
LCCN: 94-73391
ISBN 0-9636003-7-0

1. Quality control—Standards. 2. Manufactures—Quality control—Standards. 3. Total quality management. I. Title.

TS156.B43 1993   658.5'62   QBI93-21648

TABLE OF CONTENTS

Preface 4
Hints on Reading this Book 5

Text of the Standard Explained 7
Foreword 7
Introduction 7
   1   Scope 10
   2   Normative reference 11
   3   Definitions 11
   4   Quality system requirements 15
   4.1 Management responsibility 15
   4.2 Quality system 21
   4.3 Contract review 25
   4.4 Design control 29
   4.5 Document and data control 37
   4.6 Purchasing 41
   4.7 Control of customer-supplied product 47
   4.8 Product identification and traceability 49
   4.9 Process control 51
   4.10 Inspection and testing 55
   4.11 Control of inspection, measuring and test equipment 61
   4.12 Inspection and test status 67
   4.13 Control of nonconforming product 69
   4.14 Corrective and preventive action 73
   4.15 Handling, storage, packaging, preservation and delivery .. 77
   4.16 Control of quality records 81
   4.17 Internal quality audits 85
   4.18 Training 89
   4.19 Servicing 91
   4.20 Statistical Techniques 93
Summary and Afterword 95

Appendix 96
Connecting the Elements of the Standard 96
Conformance Calendar 99
Department Responsibilities 102
Scope of Registration 103
Choosing a Registration Agency 104
Related Standards 105
Comparison of ISO 9001 and ISO 9002 107
Changes Made in the 1994 Version of ISO 9001 108
The Concept of a Process 110
Hints on Writing Procedures Documents 111

Recommended Reading — Design of the Quality System 113
Total Quality Management 114
Bibliography 118
Glossary and Index 119
Corrective Action Request: 125
Summary and Structure of the ISO 9001 Standard 126

ABOUT THE AUTHOR

Leland R. Beaumont is Head of the Product Realization Process Improvement Department of AT&T Paradyne. He has lead the successful ISO 9001 compliance efforts throughout AT&T Paradyne's Design and Development organization. He has more than 20 years experience in Research and Development with AT&T Bell Laboratories, including the past six years with AT&T Paradyne. He is trained as a Quality Systems Auditor, and holds a Bachelor of Science Degree in Electrical Engineering from Lehigh University and a Master of Science Degree in Electrical Engineering from Purdue University. He is a member of the American Society for Quality Control and the Institute of Electrical and Electronics Engineers.

REGISTRATION AGENCIES

This publication is designed to provide accurate and authoritative information regarding interpretation of the ISO 9001 Standard. It is made available with the understanding that neither the author nor the publisher is engaged in rendering legal, accounting, or other professional service. If legal advice or other expert assistance is required, the services of a competent professional person should be sought. If your organization is seeking registration for compliance with the ISO 9001 Standard, contact an accredited registration agency.

RECENT REVISIONS OF THE STANDARD

This publication is based on the version of ISO 9001 that was adopted in July 1994. This is a technical revision of the original standard, adopted in 1987. Although the revisions are largely editorial in nature, some more substantive changes have been made. Refer to page 108 for a summary of the more significant changes.

ACKNOWLEDGMENTS

I want to thank Rod Goult, Ian Durand, Ed Thompson and Don Manly for helping me to understand the intent of the Standard. I want to thank all of the people who are subjected to the audits I carry out for helping me to understand the difficulties in implementing the Standard. I want to thank Ian Durand, Bob Bretherick, Curtis Redd, Don Manly, John Timson, Rusty Marr, Rosemarie J. Romanelli, Ron Schwartz, Shelly Grahek, my parents and wife for giving the manuscript a careful reading, contributing their thoughts and comments and helping to make it easier to read, more complete and more accurate. Diane McCarty did the final copyediting and typographic overview and Lloyd Delevante provided suggestions on the illustrations.

Preface

ISO 9000 is a series of documented standards prescribing quality assurance management. Written by the International Organization for Standardization, the series has been adopted by 80 countries, including the United States, Canada, the European Union and Japan. ISO 9001 has the broadest scope of these standards and is intended to be used for four purposes:

- **As guidance for quality management** — it contains useful advice for managing a business;
- **In contractual situations, between first and second parties** — it can be part of a legal contract between customers and suppliers providing the customer assurances that the supplier will carry out work in a controlled manner and that the product will consistently meet established requirements;
- **As part of a second-party approval or registration system** — a customer gives formal recognition to a supplier of conformance with the Standard;
- **In a third-party certification or registration situation** — recognized assessment firms, called registration agencies, register companies that are compliant with the Standard. This reduces the need for customers to perform assessments of their suppliers' Quality Systems. *The Standard Interpretation* concentrates on third-party registration because it is the primary use of the Standard.

The 9001 Standard presents a basic model for Quality Assurance. When requirements of the Standard are met, customers can be confident of the quality of products and services they purchase.
The ISO 9001 Standard is used in legally binding contracts, so its language must be precise. However, it must also be general enough to apply to all industries. The result is that although the Standard is fewer than ten pages long, it is difficult to read and understand. The purpose of this book is to present each paragraph of the Standard, then increase the reader's understanding with a discussion and checklist.
In its most basic form, the Standard requires that you:

- **Say what you do** — Have documented procedures for performing the work that affects product or service quality.
- **Do what you say** — Carry out the work in accordance with the written procedures.
- **Record what is done** — Retain records of activities, providing objective evidence of compliance to auditors.
- **Improve, based on results** — Compare what has actually happened to what was planned. Use this information to identify and correct shortcomings in the Quality System.

The bulk of the book is made up of units, each consisting of the following four sections:

ISO 9001 Heading

ISO 9001 Heading	**Simple Heading**
The exact text of the ISO 9001 Standard.	A simplified rephrasing of the Standard heading followed by a simplified introduction to the text of the Standard. This is intended to provide the reader with an overview of the text of the Standard.

— The Standard Interpretation

> Because simplifications and interpretations are made here, the actual text of the Standard should be referred to for critical decision-making.

Discussion: Notes on, or examples of, the best or most common practices to use in carrying out the Standard.

Checklist: A list of questions, based on this section of the Standard, that is representative of those asked by an auditor. These may be used as a checklist to assess your organization's readiness during compliance efforts or may be used as the basis for internal audits. To be in compliance, you must be able to provide objective evidence supporting a "yes" answer to any checklist question. Note that although these are valid questions and the list is intended to be comprehensive, currently no checklists are sanctioned by the International Organization for Standardization (ISO). The actual questions asked by any auditor will differ from those on this list.

Changing each question into a positive statement for action will provide a list of practical directives on how to implement each paragraph of the Standard.

Special Use Terms:

Several terms throughout the Standard have a more precise meaning than they do in common usage. They can be defined as follows:

- **Customer** — Your paying customer. The person with whom you signed the contract.
- **Supplier** — Your company. The company that employs you.
- **Sub-contractor** — A supplier, vendor or consultant to your company.
- **Shall** — You must follow this requirement to comply with the Standard.

These definitions are used throughout this book instead of the original terms. Other terms used in the Standard may be unfamiliar, and are defined in a glossary at the end of the book.

It is helpful to know that the scope of the Standard is work affecting the quality of a product or service. And the test for a sufficient Quality System is its "effectiveness." Therefore, in assessing compliance, the auditor, who is trained to evaluate compliance with the Standard, will determine whether a person's work affects product and service quality and if the Quality System is effective in preventing errors. In an effective Quality System, if errors do happen, they are quickly detected and corrected .

Interpretation of the Standard will vary from one auditor or consultant to the next and from one registration agency to the next. This book describes an interpretation based on the practices of several auditors. The exact interpretation used by any individual auditor can only be made by that auditor.

Hints on Reading this Book

The twenty elements of ISO 9001 are described in sections 4.1 through 4.20 of this book. You may read them individually in any order that is convenient. Some readers new to the Standard find it useful to start with section 4.18 and work backwards.

For each of these twenty elements, the same information is presented in five different instances in each section:

- in the illustrations,

- in the exact text of the Standard,
- in the simplified translation of the Standard,
- in the discussion, and
- in the checklist sections.

Read these in any order you like.

Novices may wish to begin by studying the figures describing each element of the Standard, then reading the table on the last page of this book to become oriented to the interrelationships between the elements of the Standard. Experienced quality professionals may wish to begin with the checklist sections. Managers may wish to begin with the discussion sections, then read the Conformance Calendar beginning on page 99. The section on ISO 9001 and Total Quality Management, beginning on page 114, will be of particular help to Senior Managers in evaluating the scope of their quality initiatives. Other individuals may wish to read in detail the paragraphs most relevant to their own work before reading the remainder of the text. For example, purchasing agents might begin by reading section 4.6, "Purchasing."

The interrelationships among the twenty elements are described in the summary and afterword on page 95, illustrated on pages 96, 97, the last page and in several of the figures used throughout the book. These elements work together to form the Quality System, and their interrelationships are important for you to understand in order to design an effective Quality System. A glossary on page 119 describes terms that may be unfamiliar or have special meaning within the Standard.

The appendix provides practical information on several topics that can help avoid problems as you undertake the compliance effort. Begin planning your activities by reading the Conformance Calendar beginning on page 99.

Text of the Standard Explained

Foreword

ISO (the International Organization for Standardization) is a worldwide federation of national standards bodies (ISO member bodies). The work of preparing International Standards is normally carried out through ISO technical committees. Each member body interested in a subject for which a technical committee has been established has the right to be represented on that committee. International organizations, governmental and non-governmental, in liaison with ISO, also take part in the work. ISO collaborates closely with the International Electrotechnical Commission (IEC) on all matters of electrotechnical standardization.

Draft International Standards adopted by the technical committees are circulated to the member bodies for voting. Publication as an International Standard requires approval by at least 75% of the member bodies casting a vote.

International Standard ISO 9001 was prepared by Technical Committee ISO/TC 176, *Quality Management and quality assurance*, Subcommittee SC 2, *Quality systems*.

This second edition cancels and replaces the first edition (ISO 9001:1987), which has been technically revised.

Annex A of this International Standard is for information only.

Introduction

Introduction

This International Standard is one of a series of three International Standards dealing with quality system requirements that can be used for external quality assurance purposes. The quality assurance models, set out in the three International Standards listed below, represent three distinct forms of quality system requirements suitable for the purpose of a supplier demonstrating its capability, and for the assessment of such supplier capability by external parties.

a) ISO 9001, *Quality system — Model for quality assurance in design, development, production, installation and servicing.*

— for use when conformance to specified requirements is to be assured by the supplier during design, development, production, installation and servicing.

Introduction

ISO 9001 is one in the ISO 9000 series of standards for Quality Assurance. Three Standards in the series can be used in legal contracts The three Standards have differing scope, with ISO 9001 being the broadest. These three Standards are:

ISO 9001 — Covers design and development, manufacturing, installation and servicing.

b) ISO 9002, *Quality systems — Model for quality assurance in production, installation and servicing.*

— For use when conformance to specified requirements is to be assured by the supplier during production, installation and servicing.

c) ISO 9003, *Quality system — Model for quality assurance in final inspection and test.*

— For use when conformance to specified requirements is to be assured by the supplier solely at final inspection and test.

It is emphasized that the quality system requirements specified in this International Standard, ISO 9002 and ISO 9003 are complementary (not alternative) to the technical (product) specified requirements. They specify requirements which determine what elements quality systems have to encompass, but it is not the purpose of these International Standards to enforce uniformity of quality systems. They are generic and independent of any specific industry or economic sector. The design and implementation of a quality system will be influenced by the varying needs of an organization, its particular objectives, the products and services supplied, and the processes and specific practices employed.

It is intended that these International Standards will be adopted in their present form, but on occasions they may need to be tailored by adding or deleting certain quality system requirements for specific contractual situations. ISO 9000-1 provides guidance on such tailoring as well as selection of the appropriate quality assurance model, *viz.* ISO 9001, ISO 9002 or ISO 9003.

ISO 9002 — Covers manufacturing, installation and servicing activities.

ISO 9003 — Covers only final inspection and test activities.

ISO 9001 is used in addition to, and not instead of, other product and service safety, performance, content or interface standards, such as Underwriters Laboratories (UL) registration, Food and Drug Administration (FDA) approvals, Federal Communications Commission (FCC) emissions standards, etc. The Standards apply equally to any industry operating in any portion of the world. The design and operation of each particular Quality System will depend on the organizational goals, nature of the business, and ways of working within each organization.

The Standard is intended to be used as is, but can occasionally be tailored for use in specific contracts. ISO 9000-1 can provide guidance in such cases.

Discussion: The ISO 9000 family contains five primary standards, ISO 9000 — 9004 and a growing number of additional standards supplementing the original five. See the "Related Standards" section on page 105 for a list of these. The specific Standard ISO 9000-1 is entitled "Guidelines for Selection and Use" and is a guide for selecting among the other standards in the ISO 9000 family. ISO 9004-1 is entitled "Quality Management and Quality System Elements — Part 1:Guidelines" and provides guidance for running your business so that it will comply with the other standards. Neither of these two "Guidelines" is to be used in contract situations or as the basis for a Quality System audit. The term "ISO 9000" is often loosely used to refer to the specific Standard — ISO 9001, 9002 or 9003 — that is of interest.

ISO 9003 is a subset of ISO 9002 which is a subset of ISO 9001. ISO 9003 is the least used standard. It applies to a company that only selects, tests and represents to its customers products designed and manufactured elsewhere. ISO 9002 is widely used and applies to companies that manufacture, install and service products designed by others. ISO 9001 is the broadest standard and it applies to companies that engage in innovative design of products or services. This book describes the ISO 9001 Standard because it is widely used and the broadest in scope.

1 Scope

1.1 Scope

This International Standard specifies quality system requirements for use where a supplier's capability to design and supply product needs to be demonstrated.

The requirements specified are aimed primarily at achieving customer satisfaction by preventing nonconformity at all stages from design through to servicing.

This international Standard is applicable in situations when

a) design is required and the product requirements are stated principally in performance terms, or they need to be established, and

b) confidence in product conformance can be attained by adequate demonstration of a supplier's capabilities in design, development, production, installation and servicing.

NOTE 1 For informative references, see annex A.

When to use ISO 9001

ISO 9001 is used when a contract, whether formally drafted by attorneys or simply an agreement of sale no matter how informal, relies on your company's ability to design a product or service, then supply and service that product. The purpose of this Standard is to assure that work is performed in accordance with specifications throughout design, development, manufacturing, installation and servicing.
Use ISO 9001 when:

a) the work to be undertaken specifically calls for innovative design because requirements are stated in terms of what the product does, rather than how it is built, and

b) your customer will have confidence in your product because you have provided assurance of your ability to design, develop, manufacture, install and service that product.

Annex A contains information that is useful, but is not a part of the Standard.

Discussion: Use ISO 9001, rather than one of the narrower standards, if your company has a role in designing the product. If your company performs product or service design work, your customer will expect it to comply with ISO 9001. See "Scope of Registration" on page 103.

Checklist: Are you registered to the appropriate Standard? Does the defined scope of your Quality System include all organizations, locations and facilities that contribute to the quality of your products and services?

2 Normative reference

Normative Reference

The following Standard contains provisions which, through reference in this text, constitute provisions of this International Standard. At the time of publication, the edition indicated was valid. All Standards are subject to revision, and parties to agreements based on this International Standard are encouraged to investigate the possibility of applying the most recent editions of the standard indicated below. Members of IEC and ISO maintain registers of currently valid International Standards.

ISO 8402:1994, Quality management and quality assurance — Vocabulary.

References in the Standard

Detailed definitions of special terms used in the Standard are defined in ISO 8402, "Quality management and quality assurance — Vocabulary" and in the specific ISO 9000 standard. These definitions are an integral part of ISO 9001. Since standards may be revised at any time, the user is advised to determine what version of each standard is current.

3 Definitions

Definitions

For the purposes of this International Standard, the definitions given in ISO 8402 and the following definitions apply.

3.1 **product**: The result of activities or processes.

NOTES

2 A product may include service, hardware, processed materials, software or a combination thereof.

3 A product can be tangible (e.g. assemblies or processed materials) or intangible (e.g. knowledge of concepts), or a combination thereof.

4 For the purpose of this International Standard, the term "product" applies to the intended product offering only and not the unintended "by-products" affecting the environment. This differs from the definition given in ISO 8402.

Definitions

The definitions given in the ISO 8402 standard apply to this Standard.

A product is the result of work activities.

Notes:

The term "product" includes physical equipment or assemblies, processed materials such as chemicals, software such as computer programs, books, or movies and is also used to mean "service".

Products can be physical or intellectual in nature.

The term "product", when used in the Standard, refers only to the product you seek to produce, and not other by-products of the production processes.

3.2 **tender:** Offer made by a supplier in response to an invitation to satisfy a contract award to provide product

The term "tender" refers to your original proposal for providing a solution to the customer.

3.3 **contract:** Agreed requirements between a supplier and customer transmitted by any means.

Any time a customer and supplier agree on requirements, a contract is established. This contract can take a variety of forms — written, oral, formal or informal.

Discussion: The glossary beginning on page 119 of this book provides definitions of the special terms used.

    The language of the Standard may lead you to believe that it applies only to manufacturing industries. However, because the word "product" also means "service", the Standard is clearly applicable to service industries. It also applies to processed materials industries and software industries, including book, movie or intellectual materials production.

Management Responsibility for Quality

4.1.1 Quality Policy:
- Defined by executive management
- Establishes objectives and commitment to quality
- Considers organizational goals and customer needs
- Understood and carried out throughout the organization.

4.1.2.1 Responsibility and authority is defined for people whose work affects product and service quality.

4.1.2.2 Adequate resources are provided, including qualified people, materials, equipment and internal quality auditors.

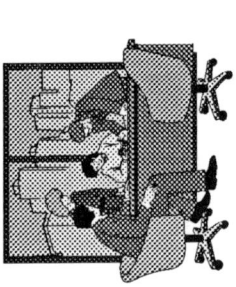

4.1.2.3 Management Representative:
- Appointed by executive management
- Ensures the requirements of ISO 9001 are met
- Reports on the performance of the Quality System
- Acts as liaison with the registration agency

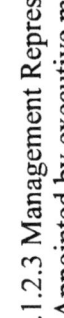

4.1.3 Executive management reviews the suitability of the Quality System:
- To ensure the continuing suitability in satisfying:
    - The ISO 9001 requirements
    - The Quality Policy
- At defined intervals
- Maintain review records (4.16)

4 Quality system requirements

4.1 Management responsibility

4.1.1 Quality policy

The supplier's management with executive responsibility shall define and document its policy for quality, including objectives for quality and commitment to quality. The quality policy shall be relevant to the supplier's organizational goals and the expectations and needs of its customers. The supplier shall ensure that this policy is understood, implemented, and maintained at all levels in the organization.

Express the Importance of Quality

The Chief Executive Officer must deploy a clearly written policy statement on the objectives for, and commitment to, product and service quality. The policy must include organizational goals for quality (i.e., aspirations for quality improvement or achievement) and support the needs of the customer.

Workers throughout the organization must understand the policy as it applies to their jobs.

Discussion: The quality policy is usually expressed as a short written statement in easy-to-understand language.

Executive Management must take a strong leadership role not only in creating the written quality policy, but in communicating it throughout the organization.

If a machine operator on the manufacturing floor were to be asked about the quality policy, the operator would not be expected to recite the policy, but would be expected to describe it in his or her own words and to know where to see or obtain a copy of the policy. The machine operator would also be expected to know how the policy affects his or her work. This might include safety practices for using the equipment, how to maintain the equipment, clear understanding of how to fabricate the product to comply with the design specifications, how to obtain help in carrying out the work, how to identify nonconforming products, what to do with them and the like.

Checklist: Is the quality policy written? Does the quality policy define the policy and objectives for quality? Does the quality policy define executive management's commitment to quality? Is the quality policy relevant to the organizational goals? Does the quality policy include reference to customers' needs and expectations? Is the quality policy authorized (e.g., signed) by the Chief Executive? Does the quality policy appear in the quality manual? Does executive management lead the communication of the quality policy throughout all levels in the organization? Do all the people in the company know where to find a copy of the quality policy? Can each person explain the quality policy in his or her own words? Can they explain how it applies to their work? Are all the people working to carry out the quality policy?

4.1.2 Organization

4.1.2.1 Responsibility and authority

The responsibility, authority, and the interrelation of all personnel who manage, perform, and verify work affecting quality shall be defined and documented, particularly for personnel who need the organizational freedom and authority to:

a) initiate action to prevent the occurrence of any nonconformities relating to product, process and quality system;

b) identify and record any problems related to the product, process and quality system;

c) initiate, recommend, or provide solutions through designated channels;

d) verify the implementation of solutions;

e) control further processing, delivery, or installation of nonconforming product until the deficiency or unsatisfactory condition has been corrected.

Organization Charts

Maintain an authorized set of procedures or job descriptions that define clear responsibilities for all people whose work affects product quality. A job description, position description, or authority and responsibility statement is required for people who:

a) take action to prevent product, process or Quality System defects, or

b) identify and record any product, process or Quality System problems, or

c) recommend or provide solutions to product, process or Quality System problems, or

d) verify that quality problems have been solved, or

e) control (e.g., stop) further work on a product until quality problems are solved.

Discussion: The itemized clauses in this section broadly refer to people whose work affects product quality, and include almost everyone in a typical company. Making responsibilities understood requires more than connecting boxes with lines on the traditional organization chart. It requires providing clear written descriptions of accountable roles and responsibilities in assuring product quality. Where job descriptions are used to establish responsibilities, they must be approved and include detailed qualification requirements for each position.

Checklist: Do job descriptions and organization charts make clear the identity, responsibilities and authority of the people who identify or take action to prevent product, process or Quality System defects (e.g., people who carry out, analyze, improve or design work processes)? of those who identify or record product, process or Quality System problems (e.g., carry out inspections or record inspection results)? Who recommend or directly solve product quality problems? Who verify that quality problems have been solved (e.g., responsible for final testing, authority to solve problems)? Who control further work on a product until quality problems are solved (e.g., authority to "stop the line" or prevent nonconforming product from being shipped)? Do people have access to these organization charts? Do people (including temporary help and contract personnel) have copies of, or access to, their own job descriptions? Do they understand their own responsibilities? Do they understand the responsibilities of those with whom they interact? Do job descriptions contain detailed qualification requirements for each position? Are job descriptions properly approved? Do personnel act in accordance with the authority and responsibilities defined in their job descriptions?

4.1.2.2 Resources

The supplier shall identify resource requirements and provide adequate resources, including the assignment of trained personnel (see 4.18) for management, performance of work and verification activities including internal quality audits.

People, Equipment and Materials

Resource requirements must be planned and provided for. This includes materials, equipment and people to manage, carry out and verify work. Resources for internal audits of work practices must be identified and assigned. People performing work must be qualified to carry out their work (see 4.18, Training).

Discussion: Management has the explicit responsibility for providing the resources required to produce quality products. These resources include qualified personnel, materials, equipment, (including inspection, measurement and test equipment), suitable working environment and time required to complete the assigned tasks. Verification activities include inspections (see 4.10), design reviews (see 4.4.6) and quality audits (see 4.17). Inspections may be replaced by other verification activities that are designed to prevent problems rather than simply detect errors.

Checklist: Have resource requirements been identified and planned? Have resources been adequately provided? Do these resource requirements include: qualified personnel to carry out management functions? Qualified personnel to carry out work operations? Qualified personnel to carry out the following verification activities: Inspection and testing of the product? Monitoring and control of the design? Of production, of installation, and of servicing? Conducting of internal quality audits? Conducting of design reviews? Are adequate resources (e.g., time, materials, equipment) available to the people who carry out the above tasks? Are the resources provided to assure product quality?

4.1.2.3 Management representative

The supplier's management with executive responsibility shall appoint a member of the supplier's own management who, irrespective of other responsibilities, shall have defined authority for

a) ensuring that a quality system is established, implemented and maintained in accordance with this International Standard, and

b) reporting on the performance of the quality system to the supplier's management for review and as a basis for improvement of the quality system

NOTE 5 The responsibility of a management representative may also include liaison with external bodies on matters relating to the supplier's quality system.

The ISO 9001 Compliance Manager

An executive appoints a manager who has the responsibility and authority to oversee and assure compliance with the ISO 9001 Standard, as follows:

a) creating and carrying out, on an ongoing basis, a Quality System throughout all organizations involved with design and development, production, installation, and servicing activities.

b) reporting to management on the effectiveness of the Quality System, to allow for its ongoing improvement.

The compliance manager is often called upon to meet with external organizations, including the registration agency and current and potential customers, to describe the Quality System.

Discussion: The Management Representative is generally a high-ranking individual, usually reporting to the Chief Executive. A written description, preferably in the quality manual, defines his or her responsibility and authority to carry out the requirements of the Standard. It is not necessary that the Management Representative devote full time to this position, as long as enough time is available to assure compliance with the Standard. The Management Representative has many duties including leading several of those activities described in the "Conformance Calendar" section beginning on page 99. The Management Representative typically sees that the following major tasks get done to gain and maintain compliance:

- Writing a quality manual and other documents necessary to a Quality System.
- Conducting internal audits, in compliance with the "Internal Audits" and "Management Review" requirements of ISO 9001.
- Contacting executive management as required to implement the Quality System, including defined management reviews.
- Requesting a "Third Party Audit" from a recognized registration agency when the results of the internal audits are satisfactory, in order to gain ISO 9001 registration.
- Preparing for and, responding to, periodic surveillance audits.
- Meeting with the registration agency and customers to describe and answer questions about the Quality System.

Checklist: Has an ISO 9001 compliance manager been appointed? Is his or her authority and responsibility defined in writing? Is this authority granted by the Chief Executive Officer? Does that defined authority include the full scope of ISO 9001 compliance? Does the compliance manager have the time, training and capability to carry out the responsibility effectively? Is this person free from any conflict of interest in carrying out the requirements of the Standard? Does the compliance manager have sufficient access to the Chief Executive to effectively carry out the responsibilities? Does the compliance manager report on the performance of the Quality System to Executive Management? Does this report include the results of the internal quality audits? Does this report include sufficient information to allow for ongoing improvement in the Quality System?

4.1.3 Management review

Top Management Reviews the Quality System

The supplier's management with executive responsibility shall review the quality system at defined intervals sufficient to ensure its continuing suitability and effectiveness in satisfying the requirements of this International Standard and the supplier's stated quality policy and objectives (see 4.1.1). Records of such reviews shall be maintained. (see 4.16).

It is the ongoing responsibility of top management to review results of internal audits (see 4.17), their ensuing corrective and preventive actions (see 4.14) and other pertinent quality-related information to ensure the continuing effectiveness of the Quality System. Records of the reviews must be kept.

Discussion: Internal audits are typically done on a rotating schedule that covers each area at least once a year. The ISO 9001 Management Representative summarizes the results of these internal audits (see 4.17) with their corrective and preventive actions (see 4.14), and reviews these results with top management. Management is also expected to review customer complaints and other pertinent quality-related data such as product return rates, manufacturing yields, warranty repair data and direct measures of customer satisfaction. Reviews are held to ensure continuing compliance with the ISO 9001 Standard, as well as the company's quality policy. Management is expected to support identified corrective and preventive actions. These reviews are held on a periodic basis (perhaps twice each year), and notes from these management reviews are kept as quality records. It is important that the outcome of the management review lead to increased effectiveness and efficiency of the Quality System.

Checklist: Are management reviews carried out? Are the reviews carried out by top management on a defined schedule? Do the reviews include an assessment of the internal audit results? Do the reviews include assessment of the effectiveness and suitability of the Quality System including reviews of corrective and preventive actions (as well as those assigned at the previous review). Are data such as customer complaints, lost customers, product return rates, manufacturing yields and other indications of customer satisfaction kept and reviewed? Are the reviews conducted using a prepared checklist to assure adequate coverage of the Quality System? Do they ensure compliance with the company's quality policy, quality manual and all elements of ISO 9001? Are the reviews conducted at a sufficiently high level in the organization to effect change? Are they conducted often enough? Do improvements occur as a result of these reviews? Are notes of these meetings available as quality records? Do they include a record of who attended, date of review, summary of information reviewed and a summary of significant action items assigned? Is the Quality System improving as a result of these Management Reviews?

Documented Quality System

This type of document . . .

A Quality Manual:
- Defines the scope of the Quality System
- Outlines documentation related to the Standard.

Documented Procedures:
- Meet all the requirements of the Standard
- Describe which tasks affecting product and service quality each process must carry out.

Optional Work Instructions:
- Describe how these tasks are to be carried out.

Quality Records result from use of the system.

Fulfills these requirements . . .

- References documented procedures (4.2).

- Referenced by the Quality Manual (4.2)
- Authorized prior to distribution (4.5)
- Defines the manner of work (4.9)

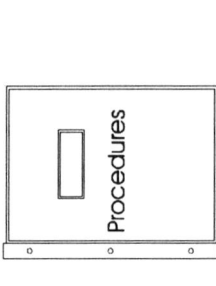

Level of detail depends on:
- Complexity of the work
- Methods used
- Skills needed, and
- Training acquired (4.2).

Collected, indexed, accessed, filed and stored in accordance with documented procedures (4.16).

4.2 Quality system

4.2 Quality system	The Approach to Quality Assurance
4.2.1 General	**Create a Quality System**
The supplier shall establish, document and maintain a quality system as a means of ensuring that product conforms to specified requirements. The supplier shall prepare a quality manual covering the requirements of this International Standard. The quality manual shall include or make reference to the quality system procedures and outline the structure of the documentation used in the quality system.	Design, and describe in writing, the company's system for assuring product quality. Write a document, called the *quality manual*, that addresses all the requirements of ISO 9001. The quality manual references the procedure documents that make up the Quality System. Keep both the quality manual and the procedures it references up to date.
NOTE 6 Guidance on quality manuals is given in ISO 10013.	More information on writing a quality manual can be found in the ISO 10013 guideline.
4.2.2 Quality system procedures The supplier shall	**Document Quality Procedures** You must:
a) prepare documented procedures consistent with the requirements of this International Standard and the supplier's quality policy, and b) effectively implement the quality system and its documented procedures.	a) Keep an updated set of documents to control and direct all work activities affecting product and service quality. b) Carry out day to day work in accordance with these documents.
For the purposes of this International Standard, the range and detail of the procedures that form part of the quality system shall be dependent upon the complexity of the work, the methods used, and the skills and training needed by personnel involved in carrying out the activity.	The extent and level of detail in the procedures will depend on the complexity of the work and the skill level of the people performing it.
NOTE 7 Documented procedures may make reference to work instructions that define how an activity is performed.	Procedure documents may reference *work instructions* that describe in more detail how to perform a specific task.
4.2.3 Quality planning	**Planning for Quality**
The supplier shall define and document how the requirements for quality will be met. Quality planning shall be consistent with all other requirements of a supplier's quality system and shall be documented in a format to suit the supplier's method of operation. The supplier shall give consideration to the following activities, as appropriate, in meeting the specified requirements for products, projects or contracts:	In creating the Quality System, consider the following suggestions:

a) the preparation of quality plans;

b) the identification and acquisition of any controls, processes, equipment (including inspection and measurement equipment), fixtures, resources and skills that may be needed to achieve the required quality;

c) ensuring the compatibility of the design, the production process, installation, servicing, inspection and test procedures and the applicable documentation;

d) the updating, as necessary, of quality control, inspection and testing techniques, including the development of new instrumentation;

e) the identification of any measurement requirement involving capability that exceeds the known state of the art, in sufficient time for the needed capability to be developed;

f) the identification of suitable verification at appropriate stages in the realization of a product;

g) the clarification of standards of acceptability for all features and requirements, including those which contain a subjective element;

h) the identification and preparation of quality records (see 4.16).

NOTE 8 The quality plans referred to [see 4.2.3a)] may be in the form of a reference to the appropriate documented procedures that form an integral part of the supplier's quality system.

a) Prepare a plan for assuring quality, if this is a job-shop situation. (See note 8 for organizations that carry out similar tasks repeatedly.)

b) Identify and acquire the resources and skills needed to achieve the required quality.

c) Ensure that documentation correctly describes each of the processes to be used and that these processes support the product design.

d) Update and improve procedures.

e) Understand the need to make measurements more precise than today's capabilities.

f) Determine how to find problems in every stage of the product development, production or installation, with emphasis on early detection.

g) Make clear the criteria to be used to accept or reject each product or feature.

h) Identify and prepare quality records.

The documented procedures making up the Quality System, as described in section 4.2.2, may serve as the "quality plan" referred to in section 4.2.3a.

Discussion: The concept of a Quality System is fundamental to the Standard and is formally defined in the glossary.

The scope of the Quality System is work that affects the quality of products or services delivered to your customer. This includes on-time delivery, correct invoicing, and resolving complaints about a product, in addition to the design and manufacture of the product.

In practice, a four-tiered system of documentation is generally used to define the Quality System. It consists of:

- A concise quality manual often 20 — 30 pages long that prescribes compliance with each of the ISO 9001 requirements as a matter of corporate policy. It also specifies responsibilities and identifies specific procedures manuals to be used in carrying out work. To illustrate compliance with the Standard and to make it readily understood by the auditors, the quality manual is best organized with the same section numbers and titles as the ISO 9001 Standard.

- A set of manuals, called procedures manuals, briefly describing the principles and strategy of each procedure. These procedures often use flowcharts to illustrate each process. See "Hints on Writing Procedure Documents" on page 111.
- A set of work instructions that describe each detailed practice making up the defined processes.
- Forms and records that result from use of the system, known as *quality records* (see 4.16)

These documents, except for the quality records, must be controlled and authorized as described in section 4.5.

Checklist: Is a quality manual written? Does it address all the paragraphs of ISO 9001? Is it authorized by the Chief Executive? Is it deployed to all personnel? Are procedures documents written for each element of the Standard that requires documented procedures? Are procedures for all work affecting product and service quality written? Are these procedure documents referenced by the quality manual? Are these procedure documents clear in their descriptions of what work operations are done, who does the work, what materials or information is required for each task, the source for each of these task inputs, what gets produced as a result of each task, the destination for each of these task outputs, the basis for making each decision described in the procedure, and the quality records to be retained? Are all these procedure documents integrated into a coherent system such that vocabulary and responsibilities are uniquely defined, conflicting roles, definitions and instructions have been eliminated and required inputs to each task are named as required outputs of preceding tasks? Are these procedure documents sufficiently clear to enable qualified workers who follow them to produce consistent products? Are the procedures documents free of subjective terms such as "as appropriate", "as needed", "immediately, "may", "often", and "sometimes"? Is daily work carried out in accordance with these written procedure documents? Is the equipment and other resources used for measurement, inspection and testing adequate? Are quality plans available for each project?

Contract Review System

Agreed requirements between a supplier and a customer, transmitted by any means

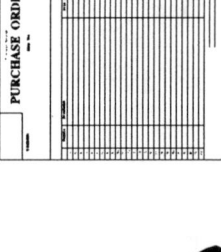

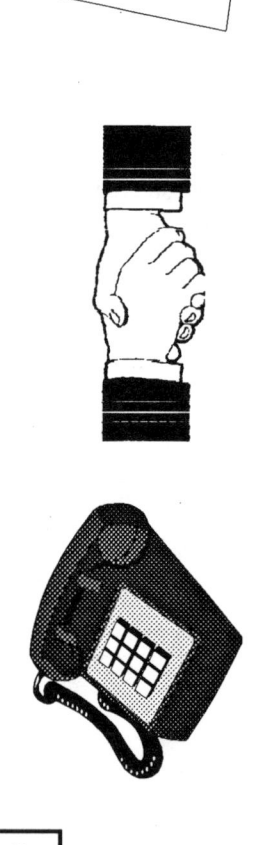

4.3.2 Reviewed to ensure that:
- Requirements are clearly defined and documented,
- Verbal order requirements are agreed before being accepted,
- Any differences from the original offer are resolved,
- You have the capability to meet the contract requirements

4.3.3 Carry out amendments to the contract in a prescribed manner and communicate the changes within your organization

4.3.4 Maintain records of contract review

4.3 Contract review

4.3.1 General

The supplier shall establish and maintain documented procedures for contract review and for the coordination of these activities.

4.3.2 Review

Before submission of a tender, or the acceptance of a contract or order (statement of requirement) the tender, contract or order shall be reviewed by the supplier to ensure that:

a) the requirements are adequately defined and documented; where no written statement of requirements is available for an order received by verbal means, the supplier shall ensure that the order requirements are agreed before their acceptance;

b) any differences between the contract or order requirements and those in the tender are resolved;

c) the supplier has the capability to meet contract or order requirements.

4.3.3 Amendment to contract

The supplier shall identify how an amendment to a contract is made and correctly transferred to functions concerned within the supplier's organization.

4.3.4 Records

Records of contract reviews shall be maintained (see 4.16).
NOTE 9 Channels for communication and interface with the customer's organization should be established.

General Requirements

Establish a procedure for reviewing the agreement of sale and any other contracts with the customer.

Review the Terms of Sale

Before offering to solve a customer's problem, or accepting a sales order, review the proposed solution or sales order to make sure that:

a) The customer requirements are defined and documented sufficiently to allow production, installation and maintenance of the products and services your customer expects to receive from you. For verbal orders, be sure the terms of the order are clear and agreed to by the customer before accepting the order.

b) It is understood where the final contract differs from the proposal.

c) You are capable of providing what has been promised to the customer.

Manage Changes to the Contract

Be precise in how to make changes to the contract, if they are required, and how to communicate those changes throughout your organization.

Records of Contract Review

Record the contract reviews as quality records.

Note: Coordinate these contract review activities with your customer.

Discussion: The intent of this requirement is "no surprises" to either your customer or the people in your company who must carry out the work of the contract through to delivery, installation and servicing of the product. The term "contract" is defined as "agreed requirements between a supplier and customer transmitted by any means". The term "contract review" refers to an examination of the agreement of sale, purchase order, verbal acceptance of a sales order, or any more formal contract between you and your customer. The term "tender" is defined as "offer made by a supplier in response to an invitation to satisfy a contract award to provide a product." Simply stated, the tender is your initial offer to satisfy the customer's request. Be clear how your final agreement (the contract) is different from the initial offer (the tender). Be sure these differences are agreed to.

Checklist: Do procedures exist for reviewing the following types of information: incoming purchase orders, sales agreements, incoming requests for proposal (RFP) or requests for quotation (RFQ), responses to RFP's or RFQ's, product or service descriptions in catalogs, advertisements, telephone solicitations, sales presentations, marketing brochures, data sheets or price lists, service agreements, and legal contracts? Is each (of the relevant above named) form of contract reviewed? Do the reviews take place before submitting a tender? Do the reviews take place before accepting an order or a contract? Are the procedures effective for both standard orders and non-standard orders? Do these review procedures ensure that customer expectations as established by the contract are clear, adequately defined and documented? Do the review procedures ensure that all requirements of the contract, including performance, quality, delivery, quantity and price, can be met? Do the procedures insure that verbally-transmitted contracts are understood and agreed to prior to being accepted? Do the procedures ensure that any differences between the initial offer to the customer and the accepted offer are understood and satisfactorily resolved? Do the review procedures insure that any differences between what the customer expects to receive and what will actually be provided are resolved with the full understanding of the customer? Are changes to the contract controlled? Do the review procedures assure that all terms and conditions of the contract can be fully met? Are amendments and other changes to the contract effectively handled? Are these changes adequately communicated within your organization? Are contract review results recorded as quality records? Are contract review activities coordinated with the customer organization? Are contract reviews effective in preventing problems?

Design Control System

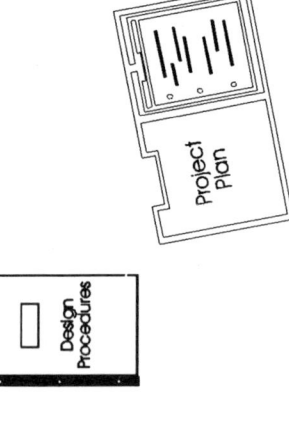

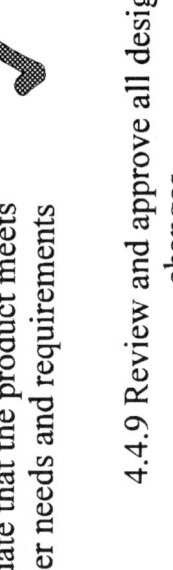

4.4.1 Carry out design projects according to established procedures

4.4.2 Plan design projects:
Assign each design and development task to qualified personnel

4.4.3 Identify the organizations involved, and describe the information flow to carry out the design project
Transmit the necessary information among organizations

4.4.4 Create clear design input requirements: written, complete, clear, reviewed

4.4.5 Create design output that meets design stage input requirements

4.4.6 Review design results with representatives concerned with the design stage

4.4.7 Verify the design to establish that design output meets design input requirements

4.4.8 Validate that the product meets defined user needs and requirements

4.4.9 Review and approve all design changes

4.4 Design control

4.4.1 General

The supplier shall establish and maintain documented procedures to control and verify the design of the product in order to ensure that the specified requirements are met.

Make Development Activities Orderly and Repeatable

Provide a design procedures manual. The design procedures must be based on fulfillment of the design specification.

Discussion: The design procedures scope begins with approval of the concept. No procedures document is required for exploratory activities, unless specifically requested in the contract. The procedures may differentiate between new product developments and product enhancements. Procedures may be established (and differ) on a per project basis.

Checklist: Does a design procedure manual exist? Does it include procedures for conducting design verification activities? Does it address all of the requirements of design control as described in sections 4.4.1 — 4.4.9?

4.4.2 Design and development planning

The supplier shall prepare plans for each design and development activity. The plans shall describe or reference these activities and define responsibility for their implementation. The design and development activities shall be assigned to qualified personnel equipped with adequate resources. The plans shall be updated, as the design evolves.

Plan Development Projects

Realistic and current plans for design and development projects must be created, documented and maintained. These plans must describe clear responsibility for carrying out each task. Assign qualified people to the design and verification work, based on their experience, education or training. Provide adequate resources to the people doing the work.

Discussion: PERT (Project Evaluation and Review Technique) charts, Gantt charts, resource requirements, task assignments and schedules, time and cost estimates are typically included in these planning documents. The plans can be revised by increasing the level of detail as the project progresses. In any case the plans are to be realistic and kept current. Make use of training records (see section 4.18) to ensure that each person is qualified for their assigned task. Provide adequate resources, including time, materials, equipment, safe work space and information to the people doing the work.

Checklist: Does a written plan, including a schedule, exist for each design and development project? Does the schedule include each design and development task? Does the schedule identify who is responsible for each design and development task? Are these resources available? Is the project schedule up to date? Do the designers have access to the schedule? Does every designer use the same version of the schedule to plan their work? Do they understand what tasks in the schedule they are assigned to carry out? Are the designers qualified to carry out the tasks assigned to them in the project schedule? Do the designers have sufficient time, materials, equipment and information to carry out their assigned tasks? Are they working according to the project schedule?

4.4.3 Organizational and technical interfaces

Organizational and technical interfaces between different groups which input into the design process shall be defined and the necessary information documented, transmitted and regularly reviewed.

Cooperate with Colleagues in Other Departments

See that design information flows between groups within design and development and between the design and development organization and marketing, sales, manufacturing, service and other organizations involved with the product.

Hold design reviews involving test, manufacturing, services, marketing and other parties with input into design and development.

Discussion: Good communication between all departments is essential for good design and development. Make sure that the test, manufacturing, purchasing, service sales and marketing organizations as well as suppliers participate as true partners throughout the design and development phase. In addition, see that these communication needs are defined, documented and effectively carried out.

Checklist: Are the roles of the people responsible for the various design-related disciplines identified for each project? Does this include test, manufacturing, purchasing, service, marketing, sales, finance and key suppliers and customers as necessary? Is the required information or other work products exchanged among these development team members? Are intradepartmental and interdepartmental work products provided to those who need them? Are design-related work products reviewed?

4.4.4 Design input

Design input requirements relating to the product, including applicable statutory and regulatory requirements, shall be identified, documented and their selection reviewed by the supplier for adequacy. Incomplete, ambiguous or conflicting requirements shall be resolved with those responsible for imposing these requirements.

Design input shall take into consideration the results of any contract review activities.

Use Requirements Documents

Write down the requirements for developing a product or service. Include government regulations and regulatory agency requirements pertinent to the product. Review the selection of features to insure they are adequate for the intended use. If you don't understand the requirements, seek clarification from the person who wrote them.

Design input requirements must be consistent with the reviewed contract (see section 4.3).

Discussion: Be sure you and your customer understand in detail what is to be designed and how it will be tested for acceptance. Use clear, written requirements. Include regulatory agency requirements. Reference or incorporate the contract or other results of the contract review activities. If this product is being developed to address a market need, rather than in response to a specific customer contract, then be accurate in representing the product to your potential customers.

Checklist: Are the design requirements for the product or service set down in writing and clearly defined? Are all applicable statutory and regulatory requirements identified? Is the definition of these design requirements consistent with the contract (see section 4.3)? Have the requirements been reviewed to ensure they are adequate for the design work to be undertaken? Have the requirements been reviewed to ensure they are adequate to meet the needs of the customer? Have incomplete, ambiguous or conflicting design requirements been discussed with the customer, clarified and removed? Do the requirements reflect the needs of the customer?

4.4.5 Design output

Design output shall be documented and expressed in terms of requirements that can be verified and validated against design input requirements.

Design output shall:

a) meet the design input requirements;
b) contain or make reference to acceptance criteria;
c) identify those characteristics of the design that are crucial to the safe and proper functioning of the product, (e.g. operating, storage, handing, maintenance and disposal requirements).

Design output documents shall be reviewed before release.

Meet Product Requirements in Final Design

The design stage results in the development of specifications known as "design output". This design output must be written with sufficient clarity to allow for checking against the design input requirements.

Design output must:

a) satisfy design input requirements,
b) specify how to determine if the product meets design output specifications,
c) highlight safety and usage considerations.

Review design output documents before using them to produce the product.

Discussion: Be sure the "blueprints" created meet customers' requirements. Be able to trace customer requirements through the entire design process.

Checklist: Are the following types of design output documented: product drawings and specifications, software (including firmware), service descriptions, and user instructions? Is the design output reviewed to verify that it meets design input requirements including all customer requirements? Does the design output include a description of how to determine if the final product is satisfactory? Are requirements for acceptance of raw materials included as part of the design output? Does the design meet all legal, safety and regulatory requirements, regardless of whether they are stated as input requirements? Does the design meet all legal and regulatory requirements for each country, state, county and city where it will be used? Does the design documentation highlight product or service characteristics that are important to the safe and proper functioning of the product or service? Does design output meet design input requirements? Has the design output been adequately reviewed before being released?

4.4.6 Design review

At appropriate stages of design, formal documented reviews of the design results shall be planned and conducted. Participants at each design review shall include representatives of all functions concerned with the design stage being reviewed, as well as other specialist personnel, as required. Records of such reviews shall be maintained, (see 4.16).

4.4.6 Review the Design

At times throughout the design process, plan and carry out formal reviews of the available design results. Each of the organizations with input into the design being reviewed must participate in the review. Record the results of each review as a quality record.

Discussion: Design reviews are defined in the glossary as: "A formal, documented, comprehensive and systematic examination of a design to evaluate the design requirements and the capability of the design to meet these requirements and to identify problems and propose solutions." They are typically conducted as a formal meeting with a standard agenda. A diverse group of reviewers, representing the many points of view pertinent to the design, are invited to participate. The design output is made available to the reviewers ahead of the review meeting to allow them time to study it. At the meeting, a moderator guides the review team systematically through the material, asking if there are any questions or issues about the current section of material. Issues that are raised are then recorded for later resolution. It is the responsibility of the design team to resolve each issue raised to the satisfaction of the review team. Although no longer required by the 1994 Standard, it is recommended that the review participants be independent of the work being reviewed to insure an objective point of view.

Checklist: Are design reviews planned at appropriate stages of the design process? Are design reviews held as planned? Are they formally documented? Are the design review records retained as quality records? Are all parties with an interest in the design output adequately represented at the reviews? Do specialists participate in design reviews when their expertise is required? Is the participation of each representative effective in assuring accuracy and sufficiency of the design output? Are identified issues tracked to verify they are adequately addressed by the final design?

4.4.7 Design verification

At appropriate stages of design, design verification shall be performed to ensure that the design stage output meets the design stage input requirements. The design verification measures shall be recorded (see 4.16).

NOTE 10 In addition to conducting design reviews (see 4.4.6) design verification may include activities such as
— performing alternative calculations,

Check the Design

Confirm at various times during the design process that the design output meets design input requirements. Record the results of these verification activities as quality records.

Use design reviews and any of the following techniques to verify the design:

— alternative theories to perform design calculations,

— comparing the new design with a similar proven design, if available,
— undertaking tests and demonstrations, and
— reviewing the design stage documents before release.

— using an existing design,
— accelerated life cycle, environmental, reliability or regulatory tests, or simulation of the equipment in operation,
— overall design review.

Discussion: Verification is defined in the glossary as: "Reviewing, inspecting, testing, checking, auditing, or otherwise establishing and documenting whether items, processes, or services, or documents conform to specified requirements." Design notebooks kept by engineers or technicians that show design calculations can be evidence of verification. These notebooks are an example of a quality record. Formal design reviews can also be used.

Checklist: Is design verification carried out? Are these design verification activities carried out at appropriate stages of the design process? Do the activities assure that the design stage output meets the design stage input requirements? Are design verification activities documented? Are design verification activities planned? Are qualified personnel assigned to these activities? Can an associated verification activity be identified for each design input requirement? Do the verification activities adequately establish that the design output meets the design input requirements? Are designs adequately verified?

4.4.8 Design validation

Design validation shall be performed to ensure that product conforms to defined user needs and/or requirements

NOTES

11   Design validation follows successful design verification (see 4.4.7)

12   Validation is normally performed under defined operating conditions.

13   Validation is normally performed on the final product, but may be necessary in earlier stages prior to product completion.

14   Multiple validations may be performed if there are different intended users.

Meet User Needs

Assure the final product meets defined user needs.

Notes:

— Achieve conformance to specification (see section 4.4.7) before undertaking design validation.

— Confirm operation under specified and controlled operating conditions.

— Confirm operation of the final product. If this is not possible, use a representative product prototype.

— Confirm operation for each intended type of user of the product.

Discussion: Whereas design *verification* compares design output to design input requirements, design *validation* ensures that the final product meets defined user needs. Field tests, beta tests or user group reaction to the pre-released product are all examples of design validations. The product must be tested under its intended operating conditions to ensure it meets the needs of each intended user.

Checklist: Are design validations being carried out? Do these validations take place after successful design verification? Does the validation take place under defined operating conditions? Are these operating conditions representative of the intended use of the product? Is the validation performed on the final product? Is the operation of the product by all intended user classes (e.g. installer, operator, administrator, service personnel, novice user, experienced user) validated? Do the validations ensure that the product conforms to defined user requirements and needs?

4.4.9 Design changes

All design changes and modifications shall be identified, documented, reviewed and approved by authorized personnel before their implementation.

Control Design Changes

Identify, document, review and approve all design changes before carrying them out.

Discussion: Design changes proposed in one component of a product should be evaluated for the effect on the whole product. The approval review typically involves the original designers. Integrate the design-change procedures into the design procedures.

Checklist: Are all design changes and modifications identified, documented, reviewed and approved? Are these changes and modifications approved by authorized personnel? Are the necessary approvals obtained before the changes are carried out? Do design changes take place in an orderly manner?

Document Control System

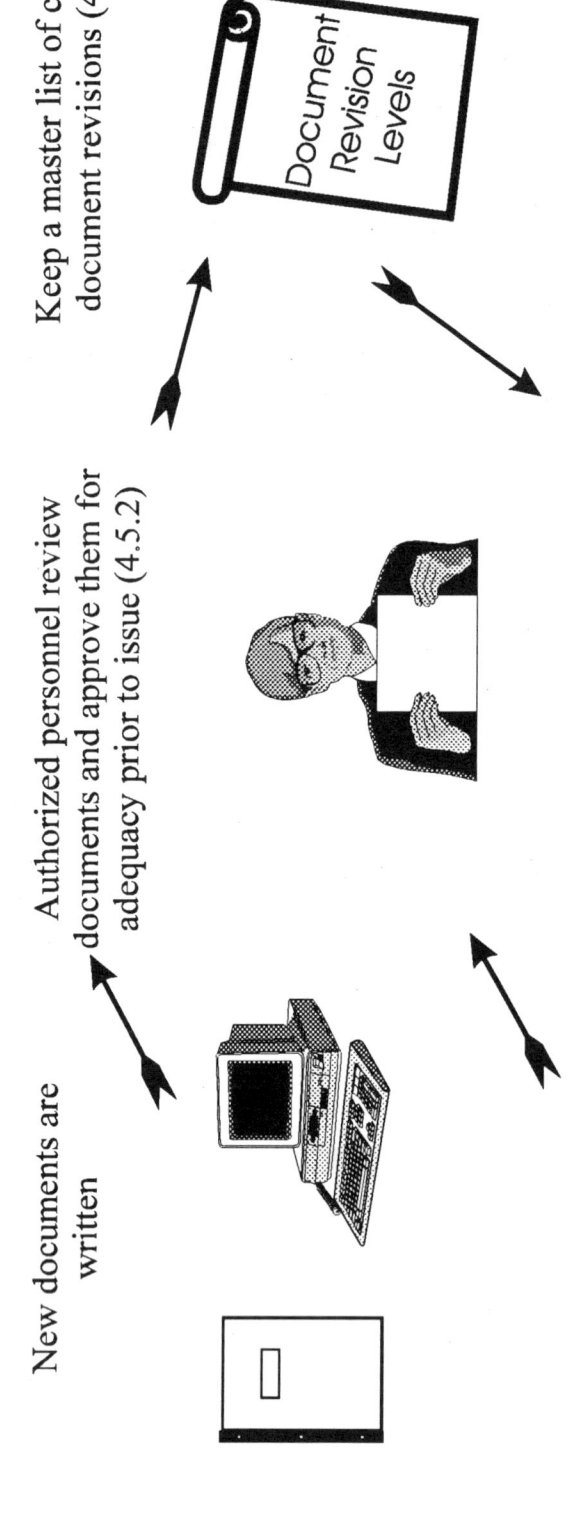

4.5 Document and data control

4.5.1 General

The supplier shall establish and maintain documented procedures to control all documents and data that relate to the requirements of this International Standard including, to the extent applicable, documents of external origin such as standards and customer drawings.

NOTE 15 Documents and data can be in the form of any type of media, such as hard copy or electronic media.

4.5.2 Document and data approval and issue

The documents and data shall be reviewed and approved for adequacy by authorized personnel prior to issue. A master list or equivalent document control procedure identifying the current revision status of documents shall be established and be readily available to preclude the use of invalid and/or obsolete documents.

This control shall ensure that:

a) the pertinent issues of appropriate documents are available at all locations where operations essential to the effective functioning of the quality system are performed;
b) invalid and/or obsolete documents are promptly removed from all points of issue or use, or otherwise assured against unintended use;
c) any obsolete documents retained for legal and/or knowledge preservation purposes are suitably identified.

Provide Workers Up-to-Date, Authoritative Documents and Data

Have written procedures that describe how to issue and change documents and other information that is used to comply with ISO 9001. Include standards documents and customer drawings within the scope of the document control system.

Note: Electronically stored information and documents are considered to be equivalent to paper documents.

Approve Documents before Use

Review and obtain final approval on documents, including procedures documents, project documents and data, before using them. Keep a controlled list of the current revision level of each controlled document. Make this master list readily available to the people doing the work.

Make sure that:

a) the people who do the work have current copies of the documents relating to work that they do;

b) out-of-date documents are removed from the workplace;

c) any obsolete documents that may be kept, are clearly marked to avoid their inadvertent use.

Discussion: If the document affects product quality, then it must be controlled. The scope of this requirement includes procedures documents, work instructions, project documents relating to a particular product, drawings, specifications and any data used to control the performance of work as well as organization charts and job descriptions. Before issuing a controlled document, review the document with people who have knowledge of the work, and authority to stipulate a process. When a new issue of a document is distributed, destroy or mark as obsolete (noting the date it was superseded) the prior issue document. Mark "Uncontrolled copy" on copies that are distributed to people for their information only and who will not be notified of document changes. A means for identifying documents and their issue status (e.g., title, and issue date or revision identifier) as well as a mechanism and authorization for review, approval, issuing and changing documents is required. An overall master list of titles is required for each type of document generate. It must be easy to determine that the documents in use throughout the entire organization are the latest version. Electronic storage, distribution and display of documents is permissible. This can greatly simplify distributing up-to-date versions of documents, but can aggravate the problem of disposing of copies printed out locally. Electronic usage, which allows printing of documents, must be carefully thought through.

The single largest source of noncompliance usually occurs with this section of the Standard.

Checklist: Are written document control procedures established? Does the scope of these procedures include control of the quality manual, all the procedure documents making up the Quality System (see 4.2), standards documents, workmanship standards and reference samples (see 4.9), materials, test software and component specifications, data used to control work operations? Are all documents making up the Quality System approved for adequacy prior to issue? Are the people who approve the documents authorized to perform such approval? Does each person doing work that affects product or service quality have copies of written procedures documents that describe their work? Are these documents the up-to-date version? Does each worker know how to determine if the document is the up-to-date version? Is a master list of documentation, including the current issue number, available? Does each worker have ready access to this master list? Does the version number of each document in use agree with the version number on the master list? Are obsolete documents (i.e., documents that have been superseded by a later version) removed from all places where they might be used? Are all obsolete documents either destroyed or suitably marked to insure they are not inadvertently used? Are documents in use free from written notes that change their meaning? Is the workplace free from uncontrolled documents in the form of informal posted notes or personal job aids?

4.5.3 Document and data changes

Changes to documents and data shall be reviewed and approved by the same functions/organizations that performed the original review and approval, unless specifically designated otherwise. The designated functions/organizations shall have access to pertinent background information upon which to base their review and approval.

Where practicable, the nature of the change shall be identified in the document or the appropriate attachments.

Control Document and Data Changes

People who are familiar with the original document should review changes to be made to that document. Provide document reviewers with the information they need to make informed decisions.

It is good to identify in writing the nature of the changes made to the revised document.

Discussion: Changing a document can affect product quality as much as issuing the original document. Therefore, the same approvals required to issue the original document are recommended to be used for issuing changes to the document.

Checklist: Are document changes and modifications subject to the same approval requirements as the original document? Is the information needed to assess the impact of proposed document changes made available to the people who approve the changes? Is the nature of the change identified on each modified document?

Purchasing System

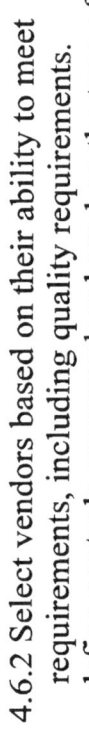

4.6.1 Purchasing procedures ensure that purchased products and services conform to requirements.

4.6.2 Select vendors based on their ability to meet requirements, including quality requirements.
- define controls over vendors based on the type of product, it's impact on the final product, and the vendor performance record.
- Maintain records of acceptable vendors.

4.6.3 Purchasing documents clearly describe the product ordered:
- Clearly specified Type, class, grade, etc.,
- Identification of product, applicable drawings, technical data, approval requirements, etc.
- Relevant quality system standard,
- Reviewed prior to release.

4.6.4 Arrangements may be made for you or your customer to verify the product at the vendor's site.

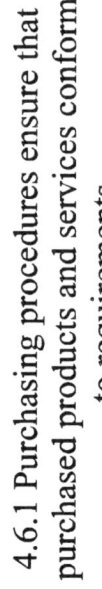

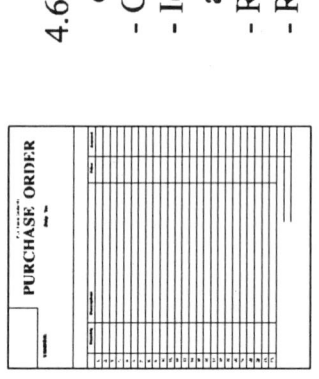

— *The Standard Interpretation*

4.6 Purchasing

4.6.1 General

The supplier shall establish and maintain documented procedures to ensure that purchased product (see 3.1) conforms to specified requirements.

Request Exactly What is Needed from Your Suppliers

Have written procedures assuring that services, hardware, processed materials and software you obtain from suppliers are precisely what you specify and need.

Discussion: The Standard recognizes that a chain is only as strong as its weakest link. Most products are assembled from materials obtained from outside suppliers. To ensure that the materials or services you purchase are suitable, this section extends your Quality System to include the selection of suppliers and the material or services purchased from them.

Checklist: Are there written procedures for the selection of subcontractors and the writing of purchase orders? Does the scope of these written procedures include all services, hardware, processed materials and software that affects the quality of products and services?

4.6.2 Evaluation of subcontractors

The supplier shall:

a) evaluate and select subcontractors on the basis of their ability to meet subcontract requirements including the quality system and quality assurance requirements;

b) define the type and extent of control exercised by the supplier over subcontractors. This shall be dependent upon the type of product, the impact of subcontracted product on the quality of final product and, where applicable, on the quality audit reports and/or quality records of subcontractors' previously demonstrated capability and performance.

c) Establish and maintain quality records of acceptable sub-contractors (see 4.16).

Manage Your Suppliers

You must:

a) Choose suppliers based on their ability to provide products that meet your specifications, especially quality requirements.

b) The degree of control you exercise over selection of suppliers depends on the type of product purchased and the suppliers' previous history of performance.

c) Establish and use lists of approved suppliers based on product quality requirements. Maintain a written quality record of your approved suppliers.

Discussion: An effective, although not yet typical, way to comply with these purchasing requirements is to have your suppliers obtain registration with the applicable ISO 9000 series standard. Consult historical information that evaluates the quality of the supplier's product. This performance history will give an indication as to whether or not quality management regarding your suppliers is effective. Institute procedures for taking corrective action with suppliers when they provide defective material or services. Be prepared, with written procedures, to remove a supplier from your approved list if they do not comply with the requested corrective action. Products or services obtained by divisions within your company that are outside your Quality System are treated as if they are provided by an outside supplier and must comply with this provision.

Checklist: Are subcontractors assessed and selected on the basis of their ability to meet your quality requirements? Are records of approved subcontractors (e.g., an approved suppliers list) kept as a quality record? Is the degree of control exercised in the selection of subcontractors based on the critical nature of the type of product or service being purchased? Is selection of subcontractors based on their previously demonstrated capability and level of performance? Are the selected suppliers effective in providing quality product?

4.6.3 Purchasing data

Purchasing documents shall contain data clearly describing the product ordered, including where applicable:

a) the type, class, grade or other precise identification;
b) the title or other positive identification, and applicable issue of specifications, drawings, process requirements, inspection instructions, and other relevant technical data, including requirements for approval or qualification of product, procedures, process equipment and personnel;
c) the title, number, and issue of the quality system standard to be applied to the product.

The supplier shall review and approve purchasing documents for adequacy of specified requirements prior to release.

Write Precise Purchase Orders

Clearly describe on purchase orders the product or service being ordered.

a) Include a precise identification of the product;

b) identify or set forth detailed specifications for the product being ordered (these may include requirements for inspection or approval);

c) point out the particular Quality System Standard (e.g., ISO 9001) that your supplier must satisfy, if any, for this product.

Review and approve purchase orders based on the above criteria before sending them out.

Discussion: Where one exists, make reference to a contract or product specification on the purchase order. Require effective review and approval of purchase orders. Consider including the following information: quantity and price, delivery date and location, identification of detailed specifications of type, class, style and grade of product including the specification issue number, performance characteristics, packaging and labeling requirements, product quality data such as inspection certification or statistical control charts, pre-shipment sample requirements, point of ownership transfer, and transportation requirements.

If the supplier is required to comply with the requirements of ISO 9001 in fulfilling the order, say so in the purchase order.

Checklist: Do purchase orders contain the following information, as applicable: type, grade or class of product, title or other identification of the product, reference to drawings, specifications, process requirements and inspection instructions including the relevant issue of each? Do purchase orders include reference to requirements for approval or qualification of the product, procedures, process equipment and personnel as applicable? Are delivery timing requirements specified? Are receiving inspection procedures coordinated with the acceptance requirements appearing on the purchase orders? Do purchase orders specify that work must be carried out in accordance with ISO 9000, or any other standard of performance, if that is what is expected? Are purchase orders reviewed and approved for adequacy of specification before being sent out? Are purchase orders clear and precise? Is satisfactory material being received?

4.6.4 Verification of purchased product

4.6.4.1 Supplier verification at subcontractor's premises

Where the supplier proposes to verify purchased product at the subcontractor's premises, the supplier shall specify verification arrangements and the method of product release in the purchasing documents.

Site Inspection

If you plan to visit your supplier's place of business to inspect the product you have purchased, then arrange for this in the purchase order.

Discussion: You may wish to avoid incoming inspection by carrying out quality assurance activities at your supplier's plant. That's permissible, but it must be specified on the purchase order.

Checklist: If purchased product is verified at the subcontractor's premises, is this specified in the purchasing documents? Is the capability of such verification consistent with the reliance placed on it (e.g., if incoming inspection is skipped based on this verification, then is it sufficient to make the incoming inspection unnecessary?)

4.6.4.2 Customer verification of subcontracted product

Where specified in the contract, the supplier's customer or the customer's representative shall be afforded the right to verify at the subcontractor's premises and the supplier's premises that subcontracted product conforms to specified requirements. Such verification shall not be used by the supplier as evidence of effective control of quality by the sub contractor

Verification by the customer shall not absolve the supplier of the responsibility to provide acceptable product nor shall it preclude subsequent rejection by the customer.

Customer Inspection of Materials

With your prior permission, your customer may verify, either at your supplier's location or at your receiving area, that material or services you purchase will provide an acceptable end product to him.

And even if your customer carries out such verification, you are still accountable for controlling the quality of materials from your supplier and providing an acceptable end product to your customer.

Discussion: There is no way around it. If you buy something which affects the quality of your product or service, you are responsible for its quality!

Checklist: If contracts with the customer provide the customer the right to verify materials at the source, is such inspection allowed? Is it specified on the purchase order? Is inspection, other than this inspection by the customer, adequate to insure the product is suitable?

Care of Customer - Supplied Product

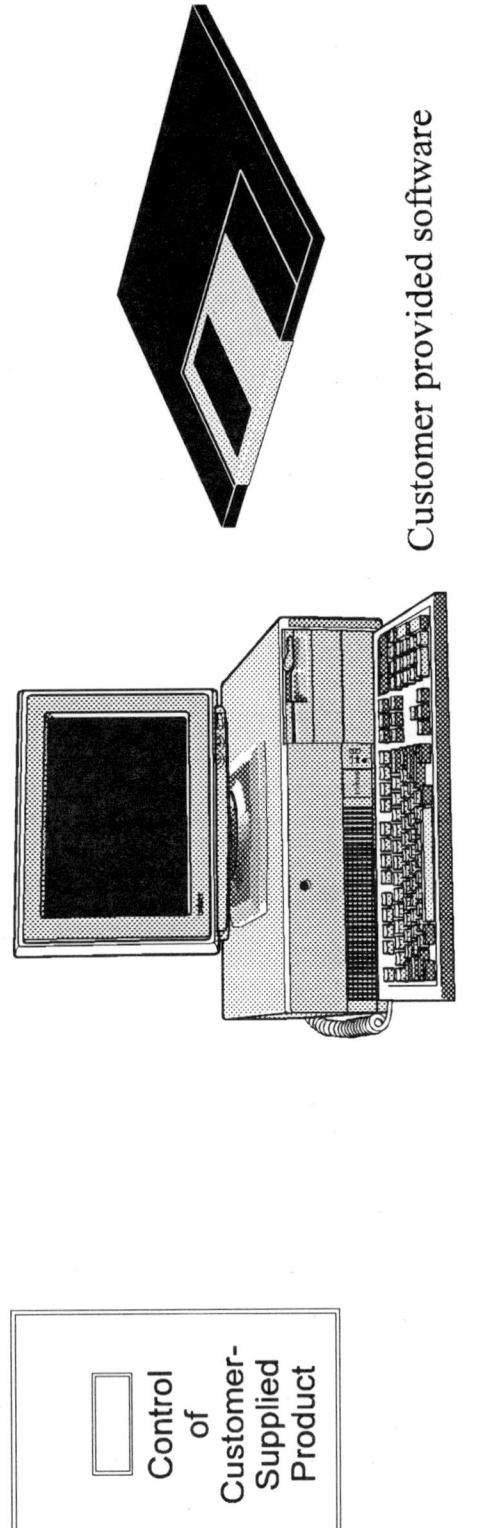

Customer provided software

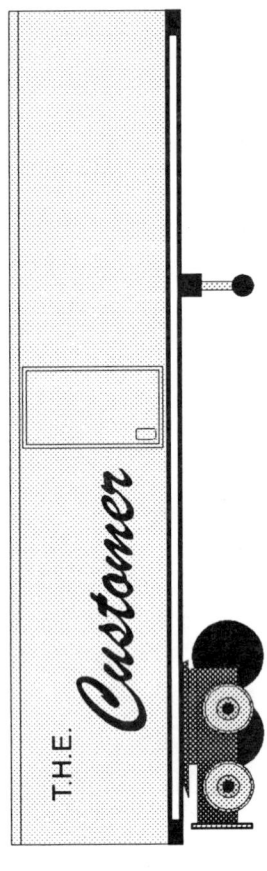

Customer-provided shipping system

Control of Customer-Supplied Product

Verify, store and maintain customer-supplied product provided for incorporation into the final product. Record and report to the customer any lost or damaged product.

4.7 Control of customer-supplied product

Control of customer-supplied product

The supplier shall establish and maintain documented procedures for the control of verification, storage, and maintenance of customer-supplied product provided for incorporation into the supplies or for related activities. Any such product that is lost, damaged, or is otherwise unsuitable for use shall be recorded and reported to the purchaser (see 4.16).

Verification by the supplier does not absolve the customer of the responsibility to provide acceptable product.

Care of Customer Supplied Materials

If your customer supplies you with materials or equipment to be incorporated into the final product, you must have written procedures that describe how to take good care of these materials or equipment. If what they have provided becomes damaged or is unsuitable for use, you must report it to the customer and a record must be kept.

The customer must provide you with acceptable product, even though you may inspect it upon receipt.

Discussion: This may include customer-supplied components such as labels, connectors, electrical components, chemical components, software modules or sub-assemblies used in the final product. Measuring instruments, fixtures, shipping containers or other tools used in construction, inspection or delivery of the product may also constitute customer-supplied equipment. It also may include customer-owned units returned for servicing or repair. This one provision is sometimes written out of a Quality System by stating that you do not accept products supplied by your customers.

Checklist: Are products or equipment provided by the customer identified? Do written procedures describe the verification, storage and maintenance requirements for these customer supplied products or equipment? Is damage or loss of this product reported to the customer? Are quality records of this loss or damage kept? Are quality records kept of loss reports made to the customer? Are quality records kept of non-conforming material supplied by the customer? If this provision is written out of the Quality System, is it assured that no such customer-supplied product is accepted?

Product Traceability System

Identify the Product from receipt and during all stages of production, delivery and installation

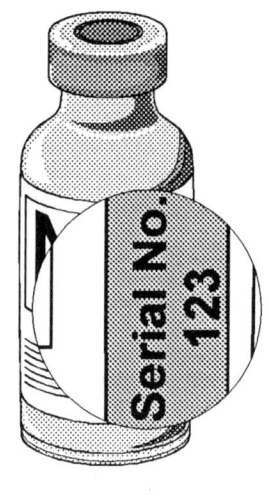

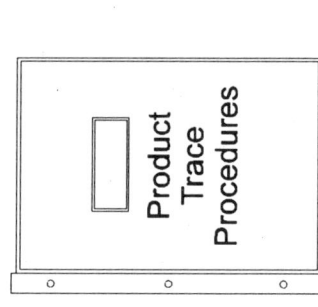

Product Trace Procedures

If required by:
- The customer
- Regulatory requirements, or
- Industry practice

Product History Trace Record

Serial No.	Batch No.	Shift	Operator	Inspector	Shipper	Hospital
123	55872	Third	Jones	Smith	UPS	Doctors
124	55873	Second	Doe	Wesson	UPS	General
125	55874	Second	Doe	Smith	FedEx	Doctors

4.8 Product identification and traceability

Product Identification and Traceability

Where appropriate, the supplier shall establish and maintain documented procedures for identifying the product by suitable means from receipt and during all stages of production, delivery, and installation.

Where and to the extent that traceability is a specified requirement, the supplier shall establish and maintain documented procedures for unique identification of individual product or batches. This identification shall be recorded (see 4.16)

Know How to Identify Products

Where appropriate, establish procedures to identify a product and determine what drawings, or other specifications, are used as it moves through manufacturing, delivery and installation.

Individual products or batches of products must also have unique serial identifications if assuring product quality necessitates this. This identification must be recorded as a quality record.

Discussion: Product identification makes it possible to distinguish one product type from another so that production personnel can determine which of several similar products they are working on. Traceability means the ability to track the history, application or location of an item or activity by means of recorded identification. Traceability produces a record of one unit's manufacturing or service history. For sensitive products, the traceability may need to begin with the receipt of raw materials and identify all intermediate stages in production. If a critical test component is found to be faulty or out of calibration, it must be possible to determine which products (either in-house or shipped) are at risk from previous use of uncalibrated equipment. (see section 4.11)

Since this paragraph begins with the phrase "where appropriate", requirements will differ by industry and by government or industry regulation agency. Traceability of items through a delivery service may also be required. Such examples include identification tags on airline baggage or identification on packages to be delivered. Consider the repair of a diamond ring as an example of a service requiring traceability. Traceability throughout the jeweler's process assures you that the diamond returned in the repaired ring is the same diamond you originally brought to the jeweler.

Checklist: Are there written procedures for maintaining product identification throughout all stages of production, delivery and installation? Is the product adequately identified in all stages of production, delivery and installation? Does this identification describe applicable drawings, specifications or other defining documents? Where required by procedure documents, customer, legal or regulatory requirements, is product traceability maintained in all phases of production, delivery and installation? Is such a product trace recorded as a quality record?

Process Control System

Carry out processes under controlled conditions:

- Suitable production, installation and servicing equipment
- Suitable working environment

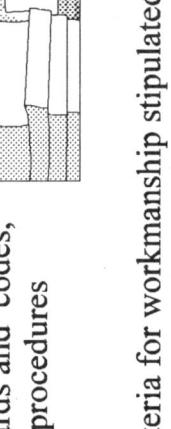

Documented procedures define the manner of production, installation and servicing

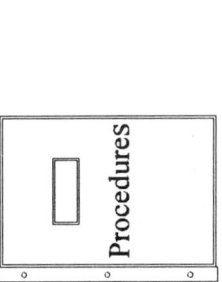

Monitoring and control of suitable process parameters and product characteristics

Compliance with:
- Reference standards and codes,
- Quality plans or procedures

Criteria for workmanship stipulated in the clearest practical manner

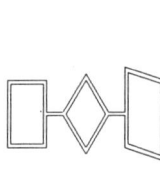

Suitable maintenance of equipment

Approval of processes and equipment

Pre-qualification of any special processes

4.9 Process control

Process Control

The supplier shall identify and plan the production, installation and servicing processes which directly affect quality and shall ensure that these processes are carried out under controlled conditions. Controlled conditions shall include the following:

a) documented procedures defining the manner of production, installation and servicing, where absence of such procedures could adversely affect quality;

b) use of suitable production, installation and servicing equipment, and a suitable working environment;

c) compliance with reference standards/codes, quality plans and /or documented procedures;

d) monitoring and control of suitable process parameters and product characteristics;

e) the approval of processes and equipment, as appropriate;

f) criteria for workmanship, which shall be stipulated, in the clearest practical manner (e.g. in written standards, representative samples or illustrations);

g) suitable maintenance of equipment to ensure continuing process capability.

Where the results of processes cannot be fully verified by subsequent inspection and testing of the product and where, for example, processing deficiencies may become apparent only after the product is in use, the processes shall be carried out by qualified operators and/or shall require continuous monitoring and control of process parameters to ensure that the specified requirements are met.

The requirements for any qualification of process operations, including associated equipment and personnel (see 4.18), shall be specified.

Provide for Orderly Manufacturing Installation and Servicing Work Flow

Plan production, installation and service processes and provide an environment in which work may proceed in an orderly fashion. These controlled conditions must include:

a) written instructions for work affecting product quality;

b) use of suitable equipment and a suitable working environment compliant with applicable health and safety standards (e.g., OSHA (Occupational and Safety Health Act));

c) adherence to applicable government, regulatory and industry standards and to your own quality plans, quality manual and documented procedures;

d) monitoring and control of manufacturing, installation and servicing operations, activities and product characteristics;

e) appropriate approval of processes and equipment used;

f) clearly expressed standards of workmanship, described in writing, by illustration or by controlled models of finished goods.

g) maintenance of equipment used in production, installation and servicing.

When the quality of work can only be verified by destructive testing or prolonged use of the product, then special attention must be paid to how the work is carried out.

Training and skill requirements for the people who carry out these special processes, as well as qualification requirements for the equipment and process used, need to be stipulated in writing.

NOTE 16 Such processes requiring pre-qualification of their process capability are frequently referred to as special processes.

These are often called special processes.

Records shall be maintained for qualified processes, equipment and personnel, as appropriate (see 4.16).

Keep records of how the work is carried out, what equipment was used and who did the work.

Discussion: Process control in a manufacturing industry usually consists of a series of measurements and inspections, carried out either continuously or as the product proceeds along the manufacturing line. Control methods also include a set of rules for adjusting the manufacturing operation (changing oven temperatures, adjusting flow rates, replenishing expended materials, replacing worn tools, etc.) in response to these measurements.

To understand the concept of process control in a service industry, consider the example of a taxi cab company. The customers need and expect a safe and courteous ride to their destination at a fair price. The process control plan for this company may require background checks, current commercial drivers licenses and specific training for cab drivers. The plan may include a daily check of mileage driven, number of customers served and total money collected. A phone number for reporting complaints might be provided allowing customers to report discourteous service. The process control plan is sufficient if it is effective in assuring product and service quality.

Process steps that affect product and service quality must be managed and carried out in accordance with documented work instructions. People doing work affecting product or service quality must be suitably qualified either by use of documented work instructions, specific training, or previously acquired skills. The product must be monitored and controlled as it flows through production processes. This may involve inspections or monitoring gauges. Equipment and processes used in manufacture must be approved for suitability. People performing production work must have a product sample or clear description of an acceptable product to use as the basis for guiding their work.

The term *special processes* typically applies to soldering, welding, painting, gluing or heat treating operations as well as cleanroom operations, sterilizing medical equipment and software development. Identify your special processes and qualify the operators of these special processes to prevent problems.

Checklist: Are production and installation processes that directly affect quality clearly identified? Are they planned (e.g., do production schedules exist for these processes)? Do documented work instructions define the production, installation and service work? Are these work instructions sufficiently clear and detailed to guide each worker in producing a uniform work result? Is the production, installation and service equipment suitable for the work being performed? Is process equipment adequately maintained to ensure continuing process capability? Is the work environment suitable? Are standards, codes, quality plans, the quality manual, documented procedures and work instructions complied with? Are production processes and product characteristics effectively monitored? Are installation processes and product characteristics effectively monitored? Are processes and equipment approved prior to being put into use? Are workmanship standards defined either by written standards or by reference samples? Are processes carried out in a controlled manner? Are any existing special processes identified? Are these identified special processes monitored or carried out in accordance with documented procedures? Is this monitoring sufficient to ensure that the specified requirements are met? Is each special process qualified to ensure it is capable of producing satisfactory results? Is the equipment used in each special process qualified? Are personnel who carry out these special processes qualified? Are records of qualification of these processes, equipment and personnel kept as quality records? Are training records of qualified personnel retained as quality records? Do the products resulting from these special processes give satisfactory performance?

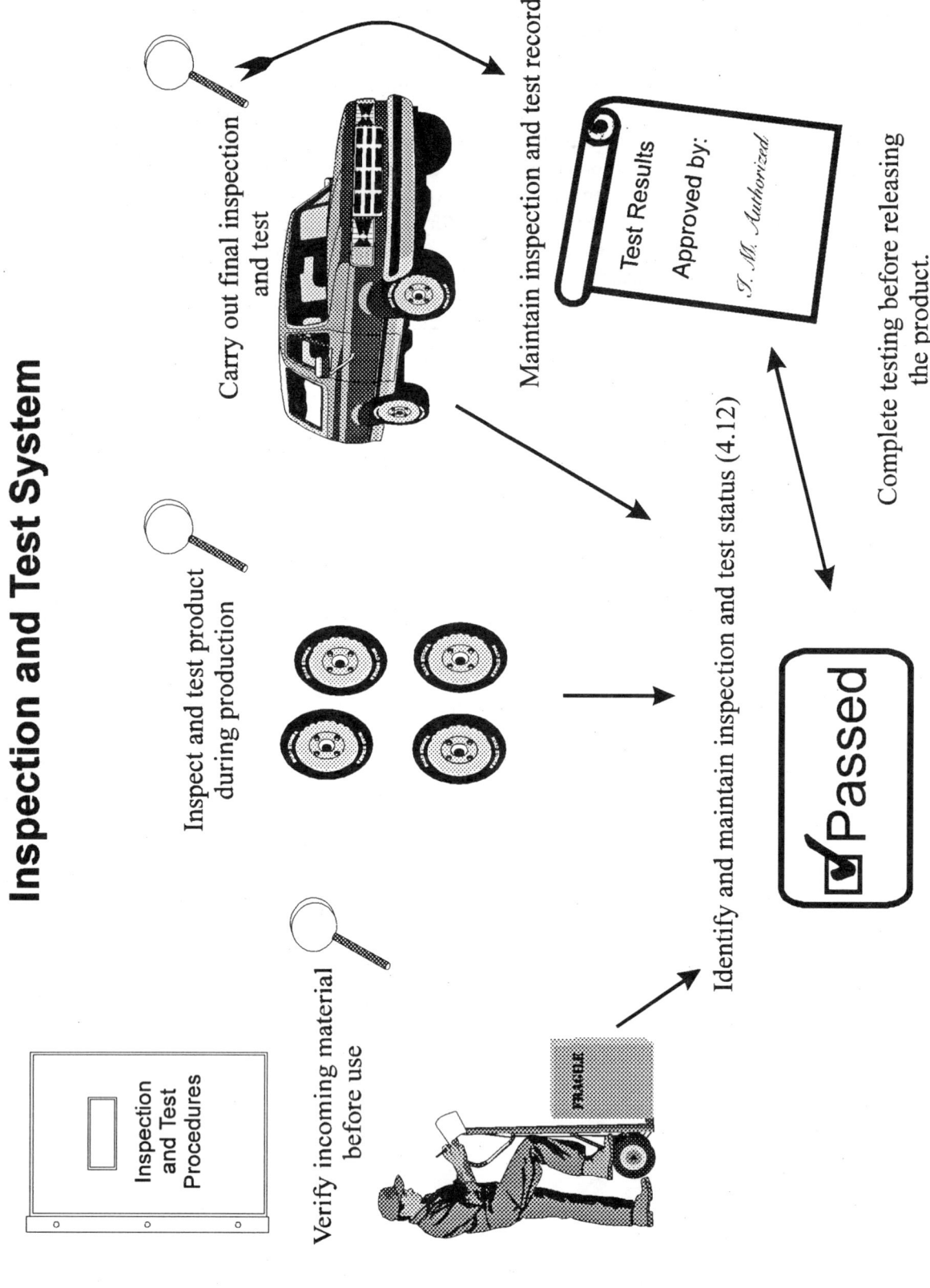

4.10 Inspection and testing

4.10.1 General

The supplier shall establish and maintain documented procedures for inspection and testing activities in order to verify that the specified requirements for the product are met. The required inspecting and testing, and the records to be established, shall be detailed in the quality plan or documented procedures.

Identify Problems as Soon as Possible

Create and maintain written procedures describing how the product is inspected and tested to assure that it meets stipulated requirements. The specific nature of the tests to be carried out and recorded must be written in either the quality plan or procedure documents.

Discussion: It is generally true that the sooner in an operation that a problem is identified and corrected, the less costly the defect will be. Design inspection and test procedures to identify problems as early as possible. In the design of your Quality System, integrate the requirements of this section with those of Purchasing (section 4.6), Inspection and test status (section 4.12), Control of nonconforming product (section 4.13) and Corrective and preventive action (section 4.14)

Checklist:: Do written inspection and test procedures exist? Are they maintained? Do the procedures describe in detail the inspection and testing activities to be carried out? Are the specified inspection and testing procedures adequate to verify that the product conforms to its specifications? Are the required inspection and test records specified in the procedure? Are inspections and tests effective in verifying conformance to specifications?

4.10.2 Receiving Inspection and Testing

4.10.2.1

The supplier shall ensure that incoming product is not used or processed (except in the circumstances described in 4.10.2.3) until it has been inspected or otherwise verified as conforming to specified requirements. Verification of conformance to the specified requirements shall be in accordance with the quality plan and/or documented procedures.

Check Out Material as You Receive it from Your Suppliers

Don't use supplies until you know they are good (i.e., meet specifications) and correct for this use. Verification of supplies must be guided by a plan or documented procedure.

Discussion: The intent of this section is to reduce the costly effects of damaged product by discovering problems as early in the operation as possible and taking steps to eliminate further damage. The scope of this section includes design and development activities, as well as production, installation and servicing. Be sure you know that incoming materials are as specified in the purchase order. Methods used to carry out this verification will vary depending on how important the supplies are to the performance of the end product and on the degree of control exercised by the supplier. Materials from approved suppliers may not need to undergo incoming inspection prior to use. Procedures should outline what corrective action is to be taken in the event faulty materials are received.

Checklist: Is incoming product inspected or verified before it is put into use? Is this verification carried out in accordance with the quality plan or documented procedures? Is the criteria for accepting incoming product clearly defined? Is this acceptance criteria consistent with the information on the purchase order (see 4.6.3)? Are receiving inspection procedures effective in detecting problems with incoming materials?

4.10.2.2 Nature of Receiving Inspection

In determining the amount and nature of receiving inspection, consideration shall be given to the amount of control exercised at the sub-contractor's premises and the recorded evidence of conformance provided.

The design of your incoming inspection procedures will depend on how reliable your supplier is in delivering quality product.

Discussion: If your supplier is diligent in assuring the quality of materials delivered to you, incoming inspections can be waived.

Checklist: Is your suppliers' Quality System, coupled with the extent of your own receiving inspection system, sufficient to ensure that incoming product meets your specifications?

4.10.2.3 Urgent Production

Where incoming product is released for urgent production purposes prior to verification, it shall be positively identified and recorded (see 4.16) in order to permit immediate recall and replacement in the event of nonconformity to specified requirements.

When operating under pressing deadlines, keep especially good records on supplies that are used before proper verification has been complete. This way they can be recalled quickly if found faulty.

Discussion: Use of supplies prior to their verification is strongly discouraged. However, if verification is not yet complete and the supplies need to be used, the Standard requires total traceability (see 4.8). Use of a quarantine area for such products is common but optional. If this procedure is ever used, take preventive action (see Section 4.14).

Checklist:: Is any material released for urgent production purposes clearly identified? Is the identification of this material kept as a quality record? Are these records sufficient to allow for immediate recall and replacement in the event a nonconformance is later identified?

4.10.3 In-Process inspection and testing

Check the Product as It is Being Made

The supplier shall:
a) inspect and test the product as required by the quality plan and/or documented procedures;

You must:
a) inspect and test the product during its manufacture, installation and servicing in accordance with documented procedures;

b) hold product until the required inspection and tests have been completed or necessary reports have been received and verified, except when product is released under positive-recall procedures (see 4.10.2.3). Release under positive recall procedures shall not preclude the activities outlined in 4.10.3 a).

b) hold the product until required inspections and tests have been performed.

Discussion: Perform tests or other verifications on subassemblies of the product while it is undergoing production. The location and frequency of checks will depend on the importance of the examined characteristics to the end product. It is permissible to allow qualified operators to inspect their own work. Document action to be taken in the event critical inspection equipment fails.

Checklist: As production, installation and servicing operations progress, is the product inspected and tested at given points as required either by the quality plan or documented procedures? Are production, installation and servicing processes monitored to ensure the product conforms to specified requirements? Is this monitoring done at points early enough in the process to avoid wasting further work on nonconforming product? Are required inspections and tests completed and the results analyzed prior to continuing processing of the product? Is nonconforming product identified?

4.10.4 Final inspection and testing

Perform Final Inspection and Test

The supplier shall carry out all final inspection and testing in accordance with the quality plan and/or documented procedures to complete the evidence of conformance of the finished product to the specified requirements.

The quality plan or documented procedures for final inspection and testing shall require that all specified inspection and tests, including those specified either on receipt of product or in-process, have been carried out and that the data meets specified requirements.

No product shall be dispatched until all the activities specified in the quality plan or documented procedures have been satisfactorily completed and the associated data and documentation is available and authorized.

Carry out final inspection and testing in accordance with the quality plan or documented procedures.

When doing the final inspection, check that all required previous tests (e.g., incoming inspection and in-process tests) have been performed and passed.

Don't ship the product until all the steps in the final inspection procedures have been successfully completed and the documentation is in order.

Discussion: Be sure to plan and carry out a specific inspection of the finished product just prior to shipment, even if many in-process inspections have already been done. If the in-process inspections are adequate, the final inspection may consist only of verifying that all prescribed interim tests were performed and passed. Decide whether to ship or hold the product based on this final inspection.

Checklist: Does the quality plan or documented procedures specify that all inspections and tests must be carried out? Does the final inspection require that all designated receiving inspections and in-process inspections were carried out? Is the acceptance criteria for each inspection and test identified and defined? Have the required inspections and tests been carried out? Is product held until all verifications, tests and inspections required in the quality plan or documented procedures are carried out, recorded and analyzed? Are the final inspections and tests effective in avoiding or detecting problems?

4.10.5 Inspection and test records

The supplier shall establish and maintain records which provide evidence that the product has been inspected and/or tested. These records shall show clearly whether the product has passed or failed the inspections and/or tests according to defined acceptance criteria. Where the product fails to pass any inspection and/or test, the procedures for control of nonconforming products shall apply (see 4.13).

Records shall identify the inspection authority responsible for the release of product (see 4.16).

Retain Product Test Records

Records of inspection and test results and acceptance criteria must be kept. The records must clearly show the pass or fail status. Failed product must be controlled as described in section 4.13, (Control of nonconforming product) of the Standard.

Record of the test results must identify who is responsible for approving release (shipping) of the product.

Discussion: Records must be kept to show that the necessary inspections have been carried out throughout the manufacture, installation and servicing of the product. As with all quality records, it must be stipulated how long such records are to be retained. This time period will depend on the service life and critical nature of the product and on specific legal requirements.

Checklist: Are records of inspections and tests kept as quality records? Do the records clearly indicate the pass/fail status of each test? Do these records include reference to the acceptance criteria used as the basis for the inspection and test? Are procedures for nonconforming product followed for all product failing tests? Are these procedures for nonconforming product consistent with section 4.13 of the Standard? Do the records identify the inspection authority responsible for releasing the product?

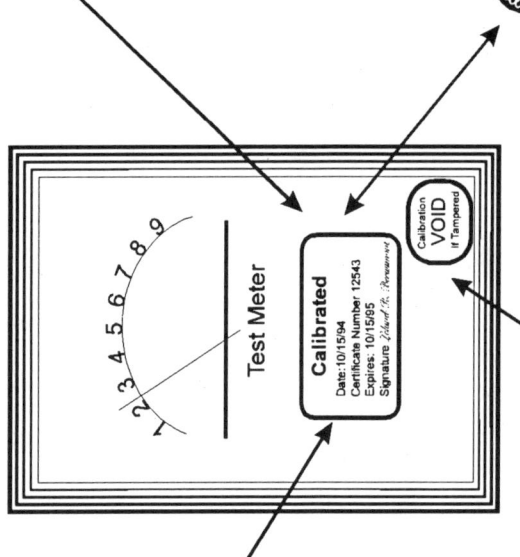

4.11 Control of inspection, measuring and test equipment

4.11.1 General

The supplier shall establish and maintain documented procedures to control, calibrate and maintain inspection, measuring and test equipment (including test software) used by the supplier to demonstrate the conformance of product to the specified requirements. Inspection, measuring and test equipment shall be used in a manner which ensures that measurement uncertainty is known and is consistent with the required measurement capability.

Where test software or comparative references such as test hardware are used as suitable forms of inspection, they shall be checked to prove that they are capable of verifying the acceptability of product, prior to release for use during production, installation, or servicing and shall be rechecked at prescribed intervals. The supplier shall establish the extent and frequency of such checks and shall maintain records as evidence of control (see 4.16).

Where the availability of technical data pertaining to the inspection, measuring and test equipment is a specified requirements, such data shall be made available, when required by the customer or customer's representative, for verification that the devices are functionally adequate.

Note 17 For the purposes of this international Standard, the term "measuring equipment" includes measurement devices.

Equipment Calibration

Written procedures must describe how to control, calibrate and maintain inspection, measuring and test equipment that is used to establish or verify product requirements. Choose equipment that is sufficiently accurate and allows the degree of measurement uncertainty to be known.

Control physical copies and versions of software and jigs used in testing products. Check them at an established frequency to ensure their proper operation and keep records of these checks.

Make measurement design data available for verification of its adequacy, as the customer may require.

The term "measuring equipment" includes measurement devices.

Discussion Compliance with the requirements of this section is particularly easy for auditors to check. The requirements for calibration are lengthy and complex so that significant diligence is necessary to achieve compliance throughout your entire organization. Include in your calibration plan small instruments and the design and development instruments where they are used to establish or verify product requirements. Also include tools owned personally by individuals performing inspection and measuring work and sensors used for process control. Label as "Calibration not Required, for Reference Only" equipment that does not need to be calibrated, either because it is not used to establish or verify requirements, or it is not designed to allow for calibration. In addition to calibrating test equipment, it is necessary to control the version of programmable test equipment software, molds or dies used to prepare samples for testing, standard color samples and any other device used for comparison as the basis of a test.

Checklist: Do written procedures exist for the control, calibration and maintenance of measuring and test equipment? Is all inspection, measuring and test equipment identified? Does this include all such equipment used in design, development, production, production control, installation and servicing? Does it include test software? Does it include all such equipment owned by the organization, on loan, provided by the customer, or owned personally by the workers? Is the measurement capability and uncertainty of each item of test equipment known? Is each item of test equipment used in a manner consistent with its measurement capability? Is test software and test hardware checked to prove it is capable of verifying the acceptability of product? Is such test software and test hardware rechecked at prescribed intervals? Is the extent and frequency of such checks established? Are quality records of such checks maintained?

4.11.2 Control procedure

The supplier shall:

a) determine the measurements to be made and the accuracy required, and select the appropriate inspection, measuring and test equipment that is capable of the necessary accuracy and precision;

b) identify all inspection, measuring and test equipment that can affect product quality, and calibrate and adjust them at prescribed intervals, or prior to use, against certified equipment having a known valid relationship to internationally or nationally recognized standards. Where no such standards exist, the basis used for calibration shall be documented;

c) define the process employed for the calibration of inspection, measuring and test equipment including details of equipment type, unique identification, location, frequency of checks, check method, acceptance criteria and the action to be taken when results are unsatisfactory;

d) identify inspection, measuring and test equipment with a suitable indicator or approved identification record to show the calibration status;

e) maintain calibration records for inspection, measuring and test equipment (see 4.16);

f) assess and document the validity of previous inspection and test results when inspection, measuring and test equipment is found to be out of calibration.

Control Procedure

You must:

a) identify the measurements to be taken, their required accuracy, and the equipment to be used to make the measurements,

b) calibrate inspection and test instruments at prescribed intervals against equipment traceable to national measurement standards (e.g., The National Institute of Standards and Technology (NIST)),

c) establish, document and maintain calibration procedures, including details of equipment type, identification number, location, frequency of checks, check method, acceptance criteria and the actions to be taken when the calibration results are unsatisfactory,

d) identify inspection equipment with a calibration sticker,

e) maintain calibration records as quality records,

f) assess and document results of using equipment later found to be out of calibration,

— The Standard Interpretation

g) ensure that the environmental conditions are suitable for the calibrations, inspections, measurements and tests being carried out;

h) ensure that the handling, preservation and storage of inspection, measuring and test equipment is such that the accuracy and fitness for use is maintained;

i) safeguard inspection, measuring and test facilities, including both test hardware and test software, from adjustments which would invalidate the calibration setting.

NOTE 18 The metrological confirmation for measuring equipment given in ISO 10012 may be used for guidance

g) use and calibrate measuring equipment in a suitable environment,

h) preserve accuracy during handling and storage of equipment,

i) prevent adjustments that would change the calibration settings.

The ISO 10012 standard provides useful guidance in designing an inspection, measurement and test system.

Discussion: The simplest approach to meeting the requirements of this section may be to employ a commercial calibration service to periodically calibrate and maintain your measurement equipment. Be sure that such a service can provide traceability to recognized national or international standards. Several services are now compliant with ISO 9000. The purchasing requirements of the Standard (section 4.6) apply to selecting and using such a service.

Checklist: Is the precision and accuracy of all such measuring and test equipment known? Are measurement requirements identified? Is the test and measurement equipment capable of making measurements to the required degree of accuracy? Is all inspection, test and measurement equipment calibrated? Is this calibration carried out at prescribed intervals or prior to use? Is the standard used for calibration traceable to nationally or internationally recognized standards (e.g., the National Institute of Standards and Technology for Quality Systems in the United States)? Do calibration procedures require a record of the equipment type, identification, number, location, frequency of checks, check method, acceptance criteria and the actions to be taken when it is determined that test equipment was used while it was out of tolerance? Are these records kept as quality records? Is it ensured that inspection, measuring and test equipment is capable of the needed accuracy and precision? Is *every* piece of inspection, test and measurement equipment identified with a suitable indicator (e.g., calibration sticker) to show its calibration status? Is the validity of previous inspection and test results assessed when equipment is found to be out of calibration? Are the nature and validity of these suspect tests documented? Are product identification and traceability sufficient to allow this assessment and possible product recall to take place? Is the environment in which the calibrations, inspections, measurements and tests are carried out suitable to obtain the required degree of accuracy and stability? Is the inspection, measuring and test equipment handled, preserved and stored so that its accuracy and fitness for use is maintained? Is the equipment safeguarded from adjustments which would invalidate the calibration setting? Is test hardware (e.g., jigs, fixtures, templates, patterns) checked to prove it is capable of performing the required verifications? Is it rechecked at prescribed intervals? Are records of these rechecks kept as quality records? Is test software controlled to assure it is capable of performing the required tests and that the current version is in use?

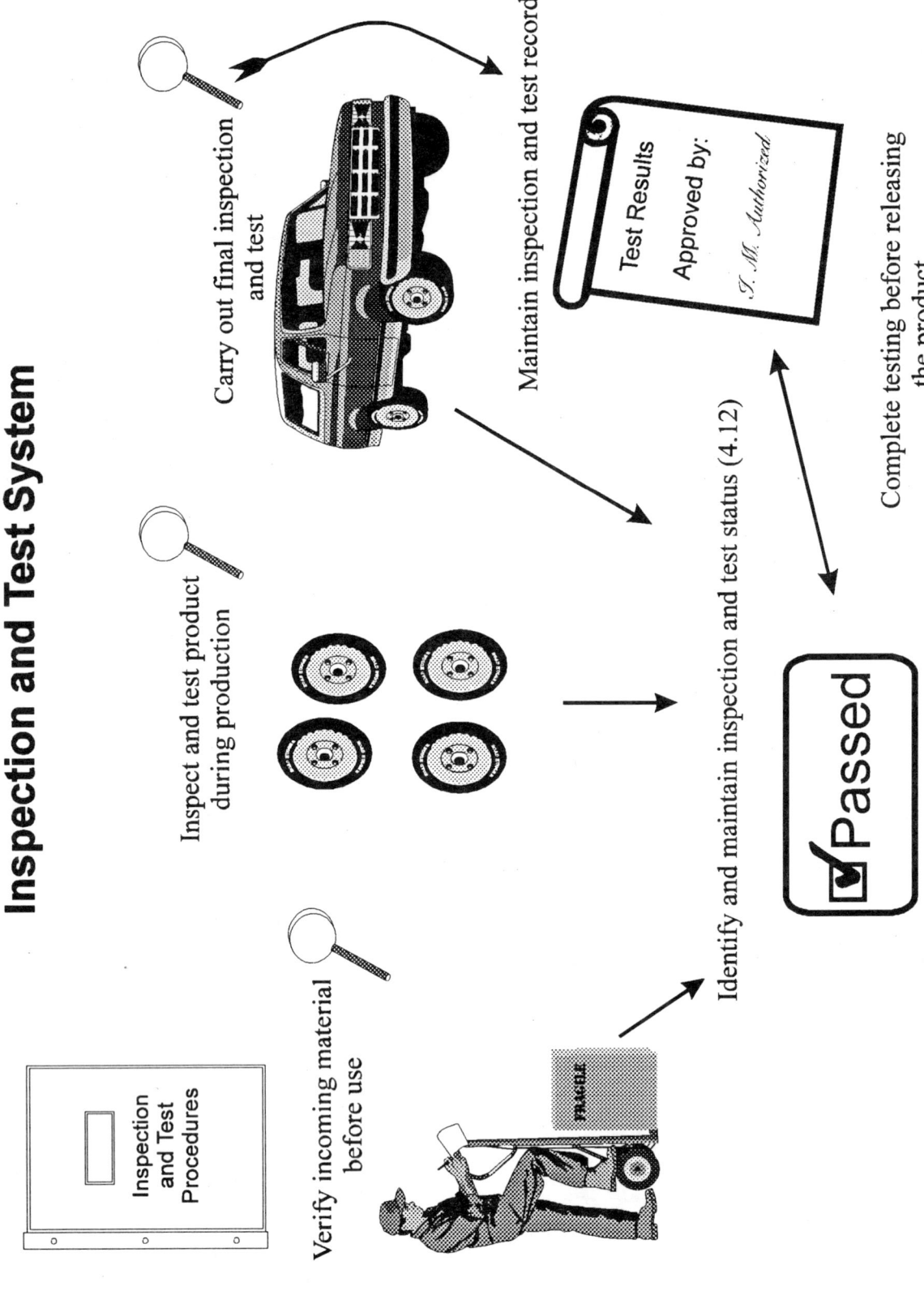

4.12 Inspection and test status

Inspection and Test Status

The inspection and test status of product shall be identified by suitable means, which indicate the conformance or nonconformance of product with regard to inspection and tests performed. The identification of inspection and test status shall be maintained, as defined in the quality plan and/or documented procedures, throughout production, installation and servicing of the product to ensure that only product that passed the required inspections and tests [or released under an authorized concession (see 4.13.2)] is dispatched, used or installed.

Mark Product as Passing or Failing Tests

Mark products after they have been inspected or tested, to identify whether they have passed, are pending results, or failed. Keep the identification with the product as it moves forward through production. Don't use a product that has failed its inspection or test.

Discussion: This requirement applies to incoming material, intermediate assemblies and finished products. Test status may be indicated by a variety of methods including the physical location of the product, notes on a routing sheet or a computer entry. Test status should be recorded in such a way that if the item gets separated from the batch, its test status can still be determined. Test status may be one of the following: not yet tested, awaiting test results, passed or failed. Record final test disposition on a quality record signed by the responsible authority.

Checklist: Is product suitably marked to identify its inspection and test status? Is this marking available for incoming material, intermediate assemblies and finished products? Is this inspection and test status indicator maintained throughout all production, installation and service processes? If traceability is required (see section 4.8), is this inspection and test status recorded as part of the traceability record? Is all product that is identified as having failed a test prevented from being dispatched, used or installed?

Handling Nonconforming Product

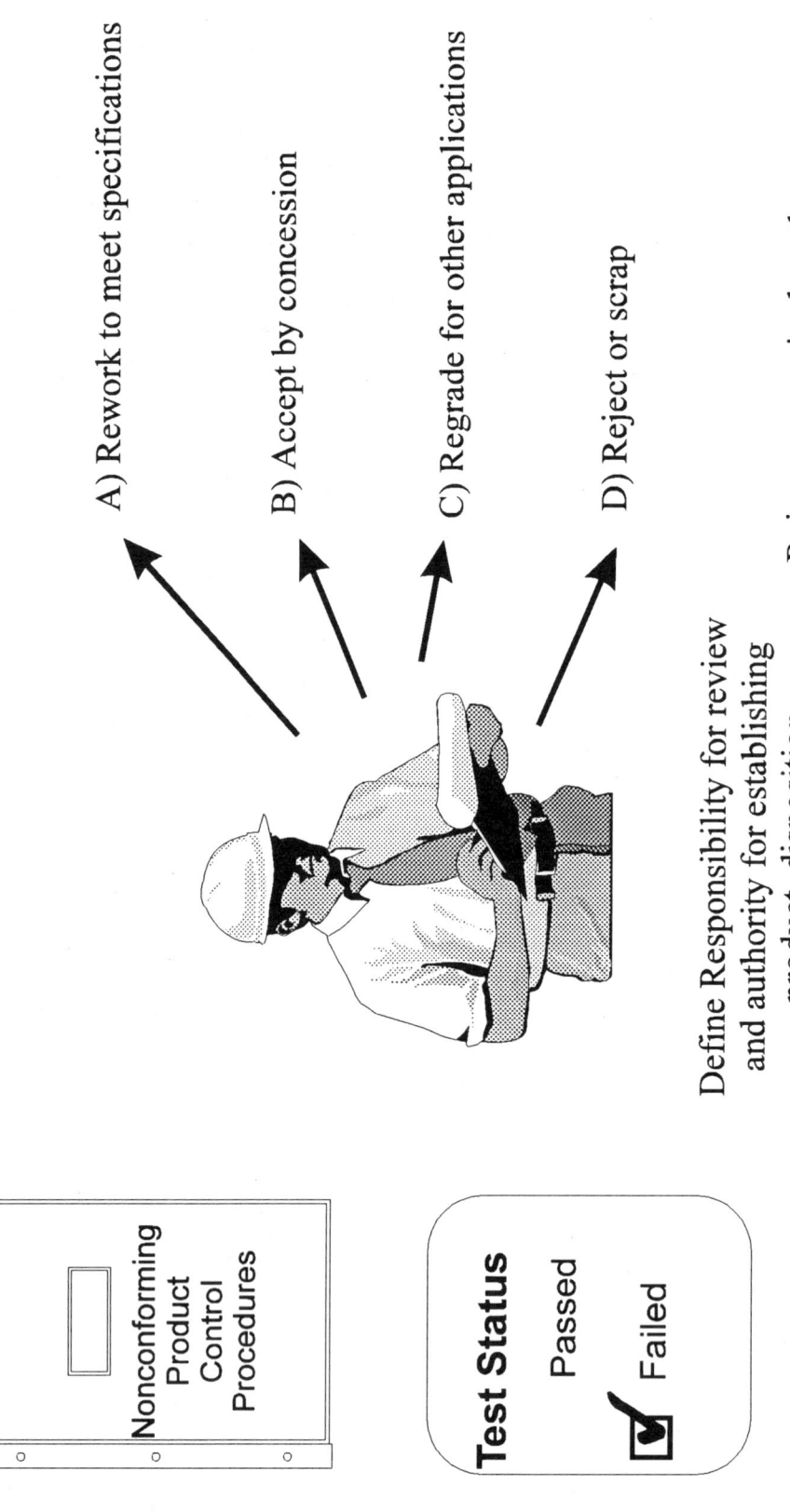

A) Rework to meet specifications

B) Accept by concession

C) Regrade for other applications

D) Reject or scrap

Define Responsibility for review and authority for establishing product disposition

- Reinspect repaired product
- Report nonconforming product as required by contract

Nonconforming Product Control Procedures

Test Status
Passed
☑ Failed

Control Nonconforming Product

4.13 Control of nonconforming product

4.13.1 General

The supplier shall establish and maintain documented procedures to ensure that product that does not conform to specified requirements is prevented from unintended use or installation. This control shall provide for identification, documentation, evaluation, segregation (when practical), disposition of nonconforming product, and for notification to the functions concerned.

Don't Use Failed Product

Have documented procedures to identify nonconforming products and make sure they are not used by accident.

Discussion: A nonconforming product is defined as any product that does not satisfy specifications as previously set forth in product requirements. Be sure to identify, document, segregate and control its further use or disposal. The system must prevent accidental use or shipment of a faulty product. Where this is impossible, agreements must be reached with the customer on the actions to be taken in case the faulty product is delivered.

Checklist: Are procedures for the control of nonconforming product written? Do these procedures prevent nonconforming product from being inadvertently used or installed? Are controls in place to identify, document, evaluate, segregate and dispose of nonconforming product? Are the people carrying out the affected functions (e.g., the next function, the end customer) notified about the nonconforming product? Is corrective action and preventive action (see 4.14) taken to prevent recurrence of nonconforming product?

4.13.2 Review and disposition of nonconforming product

The responsibility for review and authority for the disposition of nonconforming product shall be defined.
Nonconforming product shall be reviewed in accordance with documented procedures. It may be

a) reworked to meet specified requirements,
b) accepted with or without repair by concession,
c) regraded for alternative applications; or
d) rejected or scrapped.

Where required by the contract, the proposed use or repair of product [see 4.13.2 b)] which does not conform to specified requirements shall be reported for concession to the customer or customer's representative. The description of nonconformity that has been accepted, and of repairs, shall be recorded to denote the actual condition (see 4.16).

Disposing of Bad Product

Define who is responsible for deciding what to do with a bad product. Then decide between one of these four actions:

a) fix it as if the problem never happened, or
b) ask the customer to accept it, perhaps on new terms, or
c) sell it at a reduced price, or
d) throw it out or return it to the supplier.

If it is stipulated in the sales order, inform the customer whenever you have decided to repair a product. Describe and record (as a quality record) the nature of the problem and the repair steps taken.

Repaired and/or reworked product shall be re-inspected in accordance with the quality plan and/or documented procedure requirements.

Re-inspect repaired product in accordance with your procedures.

Discussion: Those responsible for deciding what to do with a failed product must be competent to evaluate the potential effects of the actions they choose. Mistakes happen. When they do, be diligent in identifying and properly disposing of the bad product. If such bad product is destined for delivery to your customer, communicate to your customer what happened.

Checklist: Is it defined who has the responsibility to review nonconforming product? Is it defined who has the authority to determine the disposition of nonconforming product? Does the scope of this definition also include nonconformities found during assembly and test? Is nonconforming product reviewed in accordance with documented procedures? Is nonconforming product assigned to one of the following dispositions: rework to meet specifications, accept by concession, re-grade, reject or scrap? Is scrap disposed of in an environmentally safe manner? Is the use or repair of nonconforming product reported to the customer when required by contract? Is repaired or reworked product re-inspected according to documented procedures? Do those procedures assure that the re-worked product fully meets the required specifications? Is nonconforming product effectively disposed of?

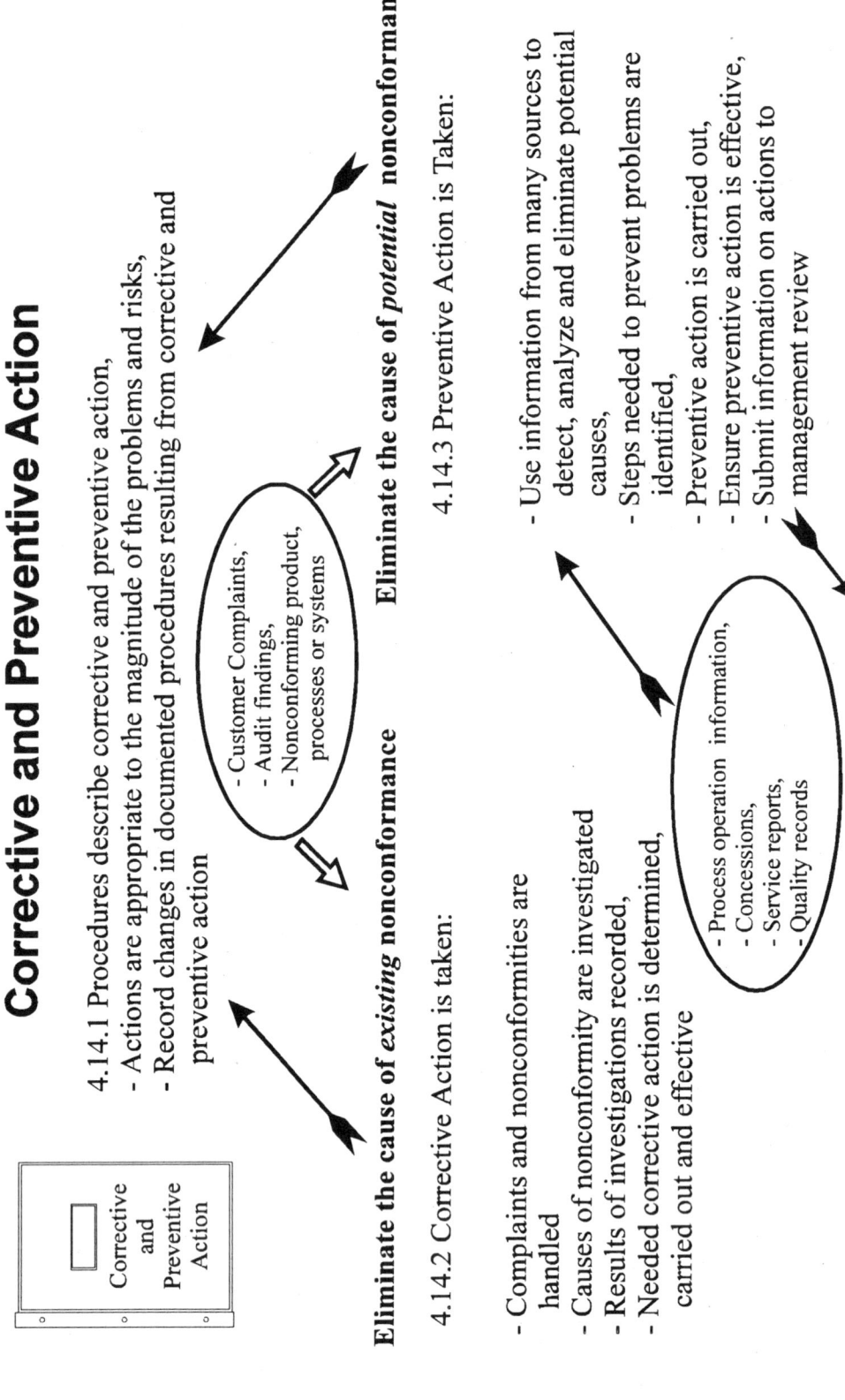

4.14 Corrective and preventive action

4.14.1 General

The supplier shall establish and maintain documented procedures for implementing corrective and preventive action.

Any correction or preventive action taken to eliminate the causes of actual or potential nonconformities shall be to a degree appropriate to the magnitude of problems and commensurate to the risks encountered.

The supplier shall implement and record any changes in the documented procedures resulting from corrective and preventive action.

4.14.2 Corrective action

The procedures for corrective action shall include:

a) the effective handling of customer complaints and reports of product nonconformities;
b) investigating the cause of nonconformities relating to product, process and quality system, and recording the results of the investigation (see 4.16);
c) determination of the corrective action needed to eliminate the cause of nonconformities;
d) application of controls to ensure that corrective action is taken and that it is effective.

4.14.3 Preventive action

The procedures for preventive action shall include:

a) the use of appropriate sources of information such as processes and work operations which affect product quality, concessions, audit results, quality records, service reports and customer complaints to detect, analyze and eliminate potential causes of nonconformities;
b) determining the steps needed to deal with any problems requiring preventive action;
c) initiating preventive action and applying controls to ensure that it is effective;
d) ensuring that relevant information on actions taken including changes to procedures is submitted for management review (see 4.1.3).

When Problems Occur, Fix the Process

Create written procedures that describe how to fix and prevent actual and potential problems.

The thoroughness of each solution depends on how costly or unsafe the actual or possible problems are.

Update documented procedures to reflect changes designed to prevent problems in operations.

Solve Existing Problems

Have procedures to address:

a) satisfying customer complaints; investigating and solving reported product problems,
b) investigating the cause of bad product, ineffective processes and failures of the Quality System; keep a quality record of each such investigation
c) understanding how to eliminate the cause of bad product
d) making sure corrective actions are carried out and that they work.

Prevent Potential Problems

Also have procedures for:

a) examining work practices, sales of known bad product, audit findings, quality records, service reports and customer complaints to identify, understand and eliminate potential causes of similar problems;
b) describing what to do to prevent any problem identified in a) above,
c) making sure preventive actions are carried out and that they work,
d) making sure that preventive actions are discussed as part of the management review (see Section 4.1.3).

Discussion: This clause requires continuous improvement of the Quality System. The phrase "corrective action" refers to eliminating the cause of a problem that has *already occurred*. The phrase "preventive action" refers to eliminating the cause of similar problems that *may occur* in the future.

A simple service example may help make this clear. In a restaurant you order a steak cooked medium rare. The steak served to you is burned. Corrective action involves giving you a new steak, and perhaps also a free dinner. Preventive action may involve improving the training given to the chef or waiter, changing procedures for maintaining or using the grill, or changing the procedures used to select steak suppliers or hire chefs.

Use of the phrase "potential nonconformities" requires preventive action be applied broadly, including diligent review and improvement of processes. It is required not only that the cause of the immediate problem be solved (corrective action) but for some types of problems, actions must also be taken to prevent similar problems from happening again (preventive action). Similar problems can be permanently prevented by identifying and correcting the root cause of the problem. Often the root cause can be determined by successively asking "why did this happen" (called the "five whys") in a non-threatening way to determine the fundamental cause for each unsatisfactory contributing condition. This will help to identify and understand increasingly useful ways to prevent related problems from occurring. Correct the root cause of the problem promptly when it is discovered.

Corrective and preventive action must investigate and address four time periods: the past, the present, the near term, and the future. Action addressing the present problem must be taken immediately to prevent further damage. Additional action must then be taken to assure that this or similar problems do not occur in the immediate future. Then consider what defective products may have been produced or delivered in the past and decide how to minimize the impact of these defects on the customer. Finally, investigate the root cause and prevent similar problems from occurring again in the future.

The following eight corrective and preventive action steps are recommended (and further described in ISO 9004, section 15): after determining what to do with the failed items, then 1) identify the problem and write a description of it using a form similar to the Corrective Action Request shown on page 125, 2) assign responsibility for taking corrective action, 3) evaluate the importance of the problem, 4) investigate possible causes of the problem, 5) analyze the problem, 6) take action to prevent recurrence of this or similar problems, 7) implement new process controls as necessary to avoid recurrence of the problem and determine the effectiveness of the change, and 8) record permanent changes in process documentation.

Checklist: Are the following types of nonconformities identified: items identified as nonconformances described in section 4.13, above, failed product, returned product, product or materials failing incoming inspection, in-process inspection or final inspection; customer complaints, warranty repairs, sales or service concessions and quality audit findings? Do procedures describe the corrective and preventive actions to be taken in each case? Do procedures require that the corrective and preventive actions taken are appropriate to the magnitude of the problem and the risks involved? Do the procedures identify which types of nonconformances are analyzed individually, which are analyzed in aggregate and which need to result in quality improvement actions? Do these procedures require that the cause of the nonconformance be determined? Do the procedures require that corrective action be taken to correct the immediate problem and eliminate the cause of actual nonconformities? Do the procedures require that preventive action be taken to eliminate the cause of potential nonconformities? Do the procedures require that steps be determined to deal with any problems requiring preventive action? Do the procedures require that preventive actions taken be reported as part of the management review? Do the procedures prescribe tracking, monitoring and other controls necessary to ensure corrective and preventive actions are taken, that the corrective actions have eliminated this type of nonconformance and that the preventive actions have eliminated similar types of nonconformances? Do workers know when to initiate Corrective Action Requests? Do workers know how to initiate Corrective Action Requests? Is it verified that corrective actions and preventive actions are effective? Do the corrective and preventive action procedures require that work instructions and procedure documents be improved to eliminate the cause of the nonconformance? Are the procedures for corrective and preventive action carried out for each type on nonconformity described above? Are problems effectively prevented?

Handling, Storage, Packaging, Preservation and Delivery

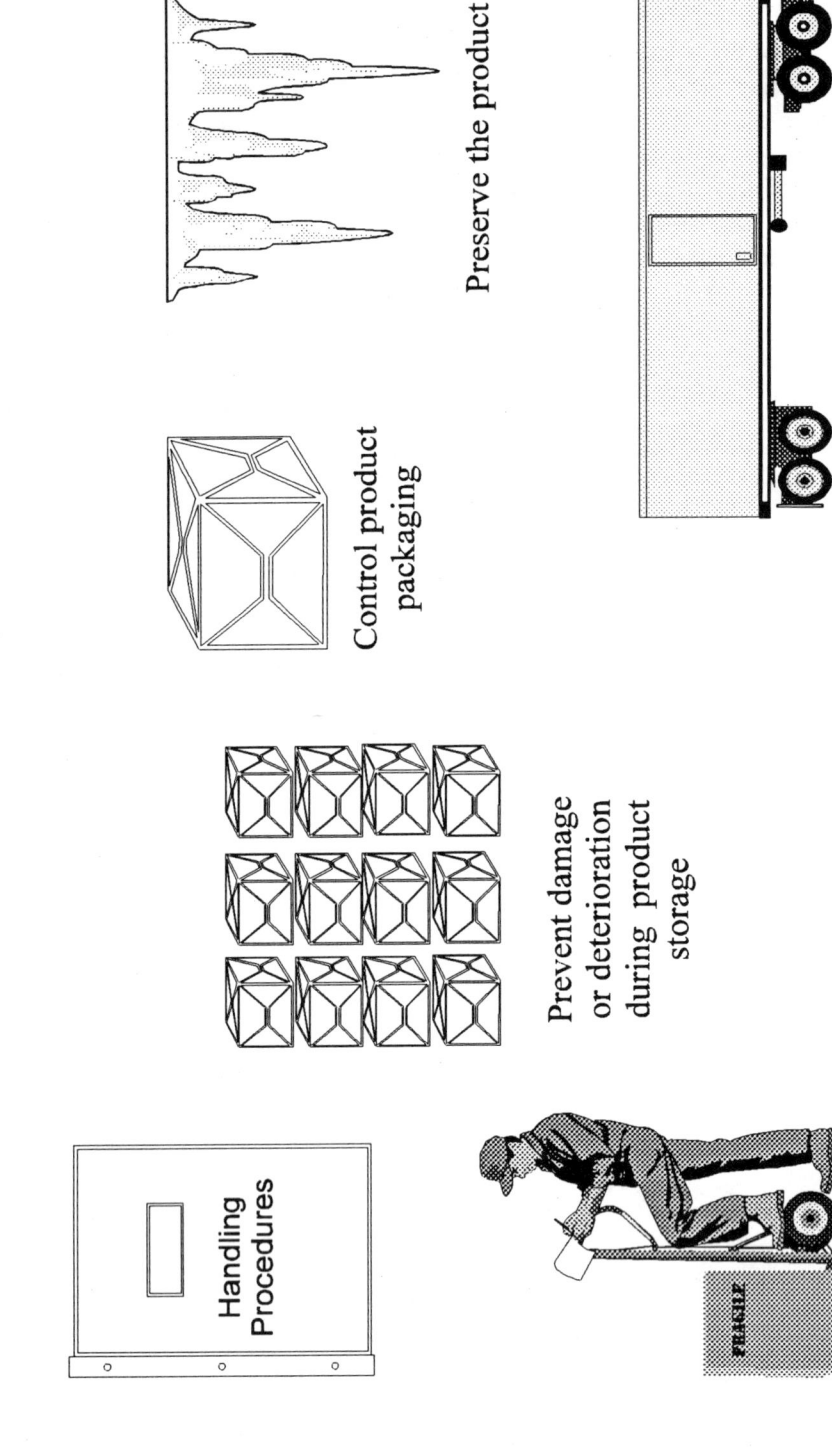

— *The Standard Interpretation*

4.15 Handling, storage, packaging, preservation and delivery

4.15.1 General

The supplier shall establish, document, and maintain procedures for handling, storage, packaging, preservation and delivery of product.

Product Preservation Procedures

Implement procedures that protect the product during handling, storage and packing, and preserve it from the time materials are received, through each intermediate manufacturing operation until the product is delivered and installed.

Discussion: The product must be protected against shipping or handling damage from the time materials are received until delivery of the final product. This includes handling of the materials and sub-assemblies during production and installation operations.

Checklist: Do written procedures exist for handling, storage, packaging, preservation and delivery? Does their scope include handling and storage of the product at all intermediate points of production and delivery? Are the procedures followed? Are they effective in avoiding product damage?

4.15.2 Handling

The supplier shall provide methods and means of handling that prevent damage or deterioration.

Handling the Product

Establish practices that provide for maintaining product quality during all handling operations.

Discussion: For sensitive electronic components, provide ESD (Electrostatic Discharge) protection procedures as necessary. For chemical products, ensure that they are not mixed or contaminated by accident, that they are not subjected to temperature extremes or other environmental conditions that would cause abnormal deterioration, and that required operations or inspections are not missed.

Checklist: Do handling procedures describe how to prevent damaging of the product? Does the scope of these procedures include handling incoming materials, and handling product through all stages of production and installation? Do the procedures prevent deterioration of the product from receipt through delivery to the customer? Do procedures for avoiding Electrostatic Discharge exist for the handling of sensitive electronic components (if any)? Do procedures protect against mechanical damage, water and humidity damage, temperature damage, corrosion and contamination? Are the handling procedures followed? Are they effective?

4.15.3 Storage

The supplier shall use designated storage areas or stock rooms to prevent damage or deterioration of product, pending use or delivery. Appropriate methods for authorizing receipt and the dispatch to and from such areas shall be stipulated.

Storing the Product

Create a secure and environmentally controlled area for storing raw materials as well as the product. Document methods for transporting materials to and from this storage area.

In order to detect deterioration, the condition of product in stock shall be assessed at appropriate intervals.

Check the stored materials from time to time to see whether they are deteriorating.

Discussion: Prevent damage or deterioration to the raw materials, intermediate assemblies and final product while it is being stored. Products and materials with limited shelf-life or special storage requirements need to be identified and stored in accordance with procedures that meet these special needs. Protect computer data files during transmission, usage and storage.

Checklist: Are the storage facilities adequate to prevent damage to incoming material, sub-assemblies or the final product? Is the storage area environment controlled sufficiently to avoid damage or deterioration of the product? Is access to these storage areas controlled? Is this control sufficient to avoid damage to stored product? Is the condition of stored material and product monitored to detect deterioration? Is material usage managed (e.g., on a first in, first out basis) in a way that prevents excessive storage times? Are computer data files protected from transmission errors, disk crashes or other events that may result in of loss of data? Does the product remain well preserved after prolonged storage?

4.15.4 Packaging

The supplier shall control packing, packaging, and marking processes (including materials used) to the extent necessary to ensure conformance to specified requirements.

Product Packaging

Control packaging, product marking procedures and packaging materials.

Discussion: The word "packaging" may refer to boxes, barrels, tank cars, oil tankers or other containers depending on what is used to transport the product. The packaging must be selected to avoid damage or deterioration of the product during its transport. Packaging requirements will differ depending on the nature of the product. For example, eggs will require more care in packing than steel bars.

Checklist: Are procedures defined for controlling packing, preservation and marking methods? Do the procedures control the storage and handling of the packing materials used? Do the procedures ensure that packaging meets contract requirements? Does packaging comply with any special requirements specified by the customer? Are instructions provided to protect the product after delivery to the customer's location?

4.15.5 Preservation

Appropriate methods for preservation and segregation of product shall be applied when such product is under the supplier's control.

Preserving the Product

Take care to ensure that the product does not spoil, deteriorate or become contaminated while in your hands.

Discussion: Keep the product safe from damage, deterioration, decay, contamination or spoilage while it is stored, shipped or under manufacture.

Checklist: Is product preserved during storage, handling and shipping? Is product prevented from contamination during storage, handling and shipping?

4.15.6 Delivery

The supplier shall arrange for the protection of the quality of the product after final inspection and test. Where contractually specified, this protection shall be extended to include delivery to destination.

Delivering the Product

Protect the product after final inspection and testing have been completed. This includes protection during shipping to the final destination, if this was promised to the customer.

Discussion: Maintain the quality of the product from the time it passes final inspection and testing until it is received by the customer. Have clear agreements with your transportation suppliers, your own transportation organization and the customer as to how each will share responsibility for maintaining product quality during shipping.

Checklist: Does a list of approved carriers exist? Are transport requirements specified for each product type? Is the protection provided during delivery sufficient to meet contractual requirements? Are responsibilities for product protection clear among your transportation suppliers, your own transportation system, and your customers? Is there evidence that handling, storage, packaging and delivery processes are effective?

Quality Records System

Demonstrates:
- Conformance to specified requirements
- Effective operation of the Quality System

- Legible
- Readily retrievable
- Protected from damage and deterioration
- Protected from loss
- Established retention times
- May be available for evaluation by the customer

May be on electronic media

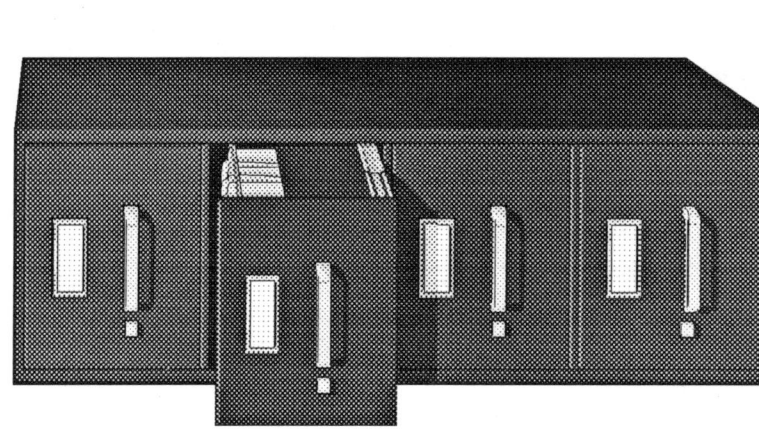

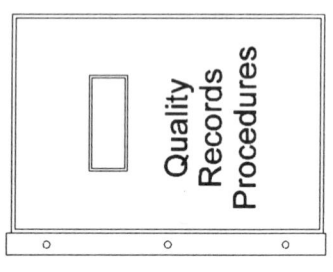

Quality Records Procedures

- Identified
- Collected
- Indexed
- Accessible
- Filed
- Stored
- Maintained
- Disposed of

4.16 Control of quality records

Control of Quality Records

The supplier shall establish and maintain documented procedures for identification, collection, indexing, access, filing, storage, maintenance, and disposition of quality records.

Quality records shall be maintained to demonstrate conformance to specified requirements and the effective operation of the quality system. Pertinent subcontractor quality records shall be an element of these data.

All quality records shall be legible and shall be stored and retained in such a way that they are readily retrievable in facilities that provide a suitable environment to prevent damage or deterioration and to prevent loss. Retention times of quality records shall be established and recorded. Where agreed contractually, quality records shall be made available for evaluation by the customer or the customer's representative for an agreed period.

Note 19 Records may be in the form of any type of media, such as hard copy or electronic media.

Maintain Records of System Use

Establish procedures for collecting, indexing, filing, accessing, maintaining and disposing of quality records.

Keep records to demonstrate achievement of requirements, and operation of the Quality System. Be sure to keep records of supplier data.

Records must be legible. Store them with retrieval and preservation needs in mind. Establish a policy for the length of time various types of records will be retained. If previously promised, the customer will have access to the records.

Records may be stored as paper, microfilm, electronically or in any other effective format.

Discussion: The Standard specifically requires (by use of the phrase "See 4.16" in each of the cited sections) retaining the following seventeen types of quality records:
- Management reviews (4.1.3)
- Contract reviews (4.3.4)
- Design reviews (4.4.6)
- Design verification measures (4.4.7)
- Acceptable suppliers (4.6.2)
- Customer-supplied product that is damaged (4.7)
- Product identification and traceability (4.8)
- Qualified processes, equipment and personnel (4.9)
- Product released for urgent production (4.10.2.3)
- Inspection and test records (4.10.5)
- Test hardware and software checks (4.11.1)
- Calibration records for test equipment (4.11.2 e)
- Review and disposition of nonconforming product (when required by contract) (4.13.2)
- Corrective action investigations (4.14.2 b)
- Internal quality audit results (4.17)
- Internal audit follow-up activities (4.17)
- Training records (4.18)

Your procedures may establish the need for additional quality records. These records must be readily accessible during design, development, manufacture, installation and servicing of the associated product. Afterwards, they can be archived to reduce storage costs. Retention times must be established.

Checklist: Do written procedures specify identification, collection, indexing, filing, storage, maintenance and disposition instructions for quality records? Are each of the seventeen types of quality records listed above kept? Are quality records, as specified in each of the procedures documents, kept? Are workers able to readily access and retrieve needed quality records? Are quality records legible? Are quality records stored in an environment that minimizes deterioration, damage and prevents loss? Are retention times established for each type of quality record? Are these retention times long enough to allow for access to quality records to verify contractual, regulatory or quality requirements? Is access to quality records provided to the customer, if it is required by contract? Are quality records disposed of when the retention time has lapsed?

Internal Audit System

- Verify whether quality activities and related results comply with planned arrangements
- Determine the effectiveness of the Quality System

Schedule on the basis of status and importance of the activity being audited

Have personnel independent of the activities carry out the audit.

Auditors:
- Observe work practices
- Examine quality records
- Identify noncompliances

Audit results are:
- Recorded
- Brought to the attention of those having responsibility for the area audited

Executive Management reviews the effectiveness of the Quality System (4.1.3)

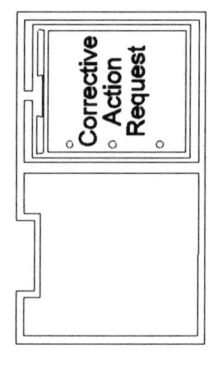

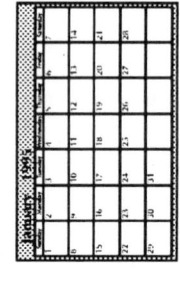

4.17 Internal quality audits

Internal Quality Audits

The supplier shall establish and maintain documented procedures for planning and implementing internal quality audits to verify whether quality activities and related results comply with planned arrangements and to determine the effectiveness of the quality system.

Internal quality audits shall be scheduled on the basis of the status and importance of the activity to be audited and shall be carried out by personnel independent of those having direct responsibility for the activity being audited.

The results of the audits shall be recorded (see 4.16) and brought to the attention of the personnel having responsibility in the area audited. The management personnel responsible for the area shall take timely corrective action on the deficiencies found during the audit (see 4.1.3).

Follow-up audit activities shall verify and record the implementation and effectiveness of the corrective action taken (see 4.16).
NOTES
20 The results of internal quality audits form an integral part of management review activities (see 4.1.3).
21 Guidance on quality system audits is given in ISO 10011.

Monitor Use of the System

Have auditors verify whether or not work activities in development, manufacturing, installation and service are being carried out in accordance with the documented Quality System.

Choose cost effective time intervals for conducting such audits, based on the importance of these activities to the quality of the product. To allow an objective evaluation, auditors must be free from influence from the activities being audited.

A written report of audit findings is to be made, with the manager of the area being audited quickly correcting any problems found.

Monitoring also includes verifying corrective action resulting from the audits.

Include a summary of audit results as part of the management review (see section 4.1.3).

The ISO 10011 standard provides useful guidance in planning and carrying out quality audits.

Discussion: Rigorous internal audits keep the Quality System alive and prevent it from becoming just another forgotten set of documents. On a planned schedule, trained auditors will read the latest version of the procedures documents that comprise the Quality System, starting with the quality manual, to determine whether it satisfies the requirements of ISO 9001. They will visit workers selected at random and ask them what work they are doing, what procedures documents they are using to guide their work, whether they have a current copy of the relevant procedures document, how they know it is the current issue, whether they have read and can demonstrate understanding of the procedures document, whether they have ready access to the required quality records resulting from use of the procedure, and what qualifies them to carry out the particular work they are performing.

The auditor will then read the procedures document and request objective evidence that each step of the process is being carried out in accordance with the procedure. Objective evidence consists of written and properly authorized (i.e., signed) forms, log entries, meeting notes or other quality records that accrue as the procedure is carried out. Noncompliance (discrepancies between the written procedure document and the observation of tasks or available objective evidence) will be witnessed and documented as it is found, using a form similar to the Corrective Action Request, shown on page 125. Each noncompliance will be cited in the audit report. The management of the group being audited is required to respond (i.e., take corrective and preventive action to solve the identified problem) to each noncompliance in a timely manner. The auditor will track the corrective action to its completion.

Checklist: Does a written procedure for conducting internal quality audits exist? Are there records showing that audits have been performed throughout all the areas making up the registration scope? Do these audits cover all twenty paragraphs of the standard over an appropriate time period? Are they of sufficient depth, frequency and detail to uncover any systematic lapses in deployment of the Quality System? Are the auditors trained to carry out audits? Are the auditors independent of the work being audited? Does a plan showing the schedule for upcoming audits exist? Are audit results kept as quality records? Is corrective action taken promptly on every deficiency found by the audit? Is this corrective action taken by the management personnel having responsibility for the area being audited? Are follow-up activities carried out to verify and record (as quality records) the implementation and effectiveness of corrective actions resulting from audits? Do the audits adequately evaluate the effectiveness of the Quality System?

Training System

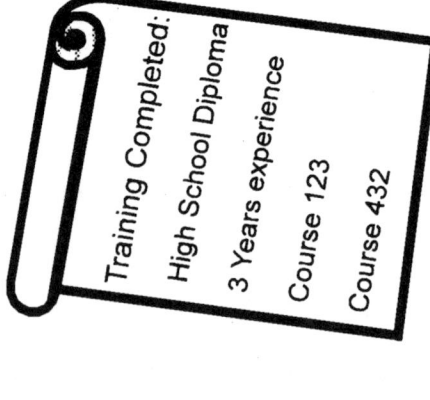

Maintain training records

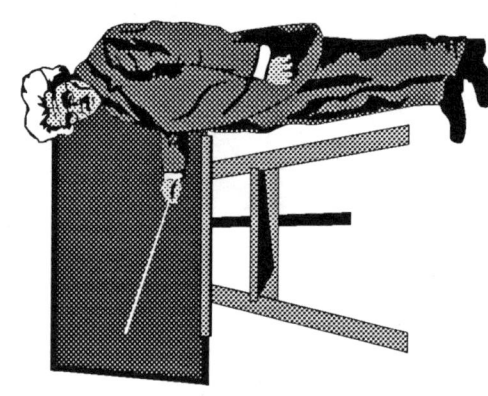

Qualify workers before assigning them to tasks

Identify Training Needs

4.18 Training

Training

The supplier shall establish and maintain documented procedures for identifying training needs and provide for the training of all personnel performing activities affecting quality. Personnel performing specific assigned tasks shall be qualified on the basis of appropriate education, training, and/or experience, as required. Appropriate records of training shall be maintained (see 4.16).

Qualify People to Do Their Job

Have a written procedure for determining what training is required by each person whose work affects product or service quality. Qualify people for their work based on their education, training or experience. Keep training records for all people.

Discussion: The point of this element is, if you are carrying out the task, you must be adequately trained for that task. This can be illustrated as follows: Imagine the next time you board a commercial airplane asking the pilot, "Are you trained to fly this airplane?" How safe would you feel if the answer were "I'm really new here, but I'm scheduled to take training next week." Or how about, "Flying seems to come pretty natural to me; I haven't had a crash yet." Or, "I'm just flying this plane temporarily while the regular pilot is out for a few days." Perhaps you would feel safe hearing, "The training classes were all full last month, and I had a rush job to complete during the only training session given this month, but I hope I'll have time next month to take the class."

Competency needs must be determined for each individual job-type based on the skills, experience and knowledge needed to perform the required tasks. An individual's competency can be established based on education, training, experience or demonstration of competency. Required training must be completed before assigning a person to carry out work. Records of training completed by each person must be kept. Training includes not only "quality related" training, but training in the technical and safety skills required to perform the work. When giving auditors access to training records, take care to maintain the privacy of personnel records by separating them from the training records.

Checklist: Does a written procedure for determining competency requirements, including training needs exist? Are competency requirements identified for each person or job category? Are these competency requirements sufficient to qualify each person to perform his or her assigned work? Do training records show that the required training has been completed by each person? Is training completed for temporary employees? Is there adequate assurance that the required training occurred and was effective? Is this assurance available where on-the-job training is used to satisfy training requirements? Is required training completed before a person is assigned to a task? Are people competent to carry out their assigned tasks?

Servicing System

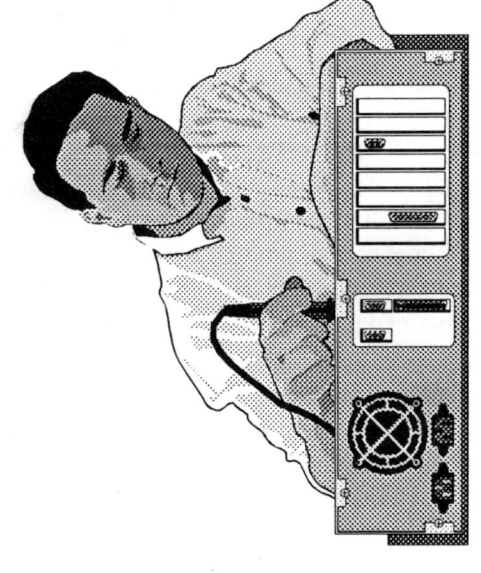

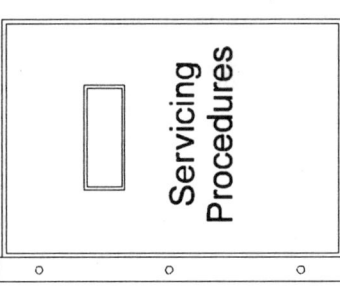

Servicing Procedures

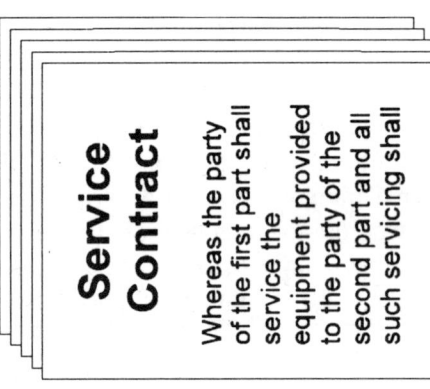

Service Contract

Whereas the party of the first part shall service the equipment provided to the party of the second part and all such servicing shall

Perform, verify and report servicing to meet specified servicing requirements.

— The Standard Interpretation

4.19 Servicing

Servicing

Where servicing is a specified requirement, the supplier shall establish and maintain documented procedures for performing, verifying and reporting that the services meets the specified requirements.

Support the Product as Promised

Have written procedures for providing customer support as promised.

Discussion: Servicing refers to support of the product after it is sold and installed. If the customer has been promised servicing, the service work must be performed in accordance with the requirements of this entire Standard and in fulfillment of the service agreement described in the contract. In short, this Standard applies as much to the customer service organization as it does to the manufacturing organization.

Checklist: Are there written servicing procedures to cover each specified servicing requirement? Is servicing work carried out in accordance with each of the twenty paragraphs of the ISO 9001 requirements? Is servicing work carried out in accordance with the servicing contract?

Statistical Techniques

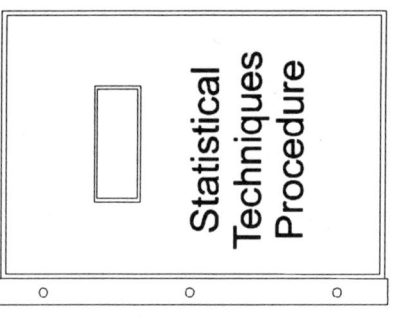

Carry out and control the application of identified statistical techniques

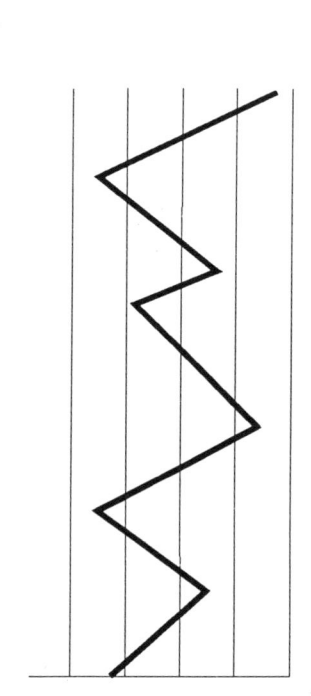

Identify the need for statistical techniques to establish, control and verify process capability and product characteristics

4.20 Statistical Techniques

4.20.1 Identification of need

The supplier shall identify the need for statistical techniques required for establishing, controlling and verifying process capability and product characteristics.

Identify Where Statistical Controls are Necessary

Identify where statistical procedures need to be used. This may include verifying or controlling processes or product characteristics.

Discussion: If you use procedures such as statistical process control (SPC) or statistical acceptance sampling, identify where such use is required. You can expect the auditor to ask about their validity. Note that this does not require the use of SPC or any statistical techniques.

Checklist: Is each occurrence where statistics are used for verifying process capability and product characteristics identified? Is the person who establishes the need for statistical control qualified to assess that need?

4.20.2 Procedures

The supplier shall establish and maintain documented procedures to implement and control the application of the statistical techniques identified in 4.20.1

Procedures for Using Statistical Controls

If statistics are used to control product-affecting processes, the statistical techniques must be valid and procedures for their use must exist.

Discussion: When statistical techniques are required to be used, they must be carried out according to documented procedures.

Checklist: In each case identified in section 4.20.,1 above, is it assured that the statistical technique being used is valid? Is each such use of statistical technique described in a written procedure? Is that author of each statistical control procedure qualified to specify the use of statistics? Where Statistical Process Control (SPC) charts are used, are the actions to be taken in response to out-of-control occurrences clearly documented? Are these actions taken? Are the statistical procedures in use providing effective process control?

Annex A
(informative)

Bibliography

ISO 9000-1: 1994 *Quality management and quality assurance standards — Part 1: Guidelines for selection and use.*

ISO 9000-2:1993 *Quality management and quality assurance standards — Part 2: Generic guidelines for the application of ISO 9001, ISO 9002 and ISO 9003.*

ISO 9000-3:1991 *Quality management and quality assurance standards — Part 3: Guidelines for the application of ISO 9001 to the development, supply and maintenance of software.*

ISO 9002:1994 *Quality system — model for quality assurance in production, installation and servicing.*

ISO 9003:1993 *Quality Systems — Model for quality assurance in final inspection and test.*

ISO 10011-1: 1990 *Guidelines for auditing quality systems. Part 1: Auditing.*

ISO 10011-2: 1991 *Guidelines for auditing quality systems. Part 2: Qualification criteria for quality systems auditors.*

ISO 10011-3: 1991 *Guidelines of auditing quality systems. Part 3: Management of audit programs.*

ISO 10012-1: 1992 *Quality assurance requirements for measuring equipment — Part 1: Metrological confirmation system for measuring equipment.*

ISO 10013:—[1] *Guidelines for developing quality manuals.*

ISO/TR 13425:—[1] *Guidelines for the selection of statistical methods in standardization and specification.*

---

[1] To be published

Summary and Afterword

The twenty paragraphs, 4.1 through 4.20, of the Standard are interrelated and form a Quality Assurance System. The table on the last page of this book is an overview of those paragraphs, showing how they support each other. The figures on pages 97 and 98 illustrate the interrelationships between several elements.

It is vital that top management actively support the achievement of product and service quality by creating and deploying a written quality policy; defining the organization and structure of staff responsible for product and service quality; providing for inspectors, independent auditors and reviewers; assigning an ISO 9001 Management Representative with the authority to carry out the requirements of the Standard, and personally reviewing the results of the internal audits.

A Quality System is created and maintained by keeping a comprehensive set of controlled procedures documents, and having the resources needed to achieve quality.

All phases of product design, development, manufacture, installation and service, from review of the sales agreement with the customer, through all intermediate stages of product design, selection and control of suppliers, identifying, testing and controlling the product during its creation, handling, storage, packaging and delivery and providing customer service, are carried out with care for product and service quality.

Work that affects product and service quality is conducted through controlled processes. This requires that the processes are effectively managed by establishing defined procedures, controlling documentation, maintaining records of results and authorizations, auditing the Quality System to keep it current, taking corrective and preventive action, calibrating measuring and test equipment and using only valid statistical techniques.

To allow all of this to happen, people are qualified to carry out their work based on their education, training or experience.

ISO 9001 presents a basic model for quality assurance. I hope this book helps you to understand and appreciate the Standard. Deciding to obtain registration is an excellent next step, or first step, in your quality journey. I hope you will take that step, it is well within your reach.

When you do obtain registration, please tell me your experiences. Let me know how this book was most helpful and where it can be improved.

Leland R. Beaumont

January 8, 1995

Appendix

Connecting the Elements of the Standard

The twenty elements of the Standard can be thought of as pertaining to one of three major sub-systems present in any corporation. These are the major processes of:

- Selling, manufacturing and installing a product or service,
- Designing and developing new products or services, and
- Improving the Quality System.

The figure "production system" on the following page shows how many elements of the Standard interrelate to assure quality during the selling, manufacturing and installing of a product or service. The process begins when a customer requests the purchase of a product or service. Prior to the acceptance of the sale, the contract establishing the conditions of the sale is reviewed. Materials are then obtained from the suppliers and the product is built and inspected using calibrated test equipment. The results of these inspections are recorded. Any nonconforming products or services are controlled, and corrective and preventive action is taken The product is protected during shipping. The product is installed and if necessary, it is serviced.

The figure "Design Control System" on page 28 shows how the sub-elements of section 4.4 of the Standard work to assure the quality of new product design and development.

The figure "Quality Improvement System" on page 98 shows how many elements of the Standard interrelate to improve the Quality System. Customer complaints, nonconforming product identified during production, and audit findings all stimulate corrective action to be taken. In addition, information from process operations, concessions, service reports and quality records is analyzed to eliminate potential causes of nonconformance. Changes are recorded in documented procedures and document changes are controlled. Finally, Executive Management reviews the effectiveness of the Quality System.

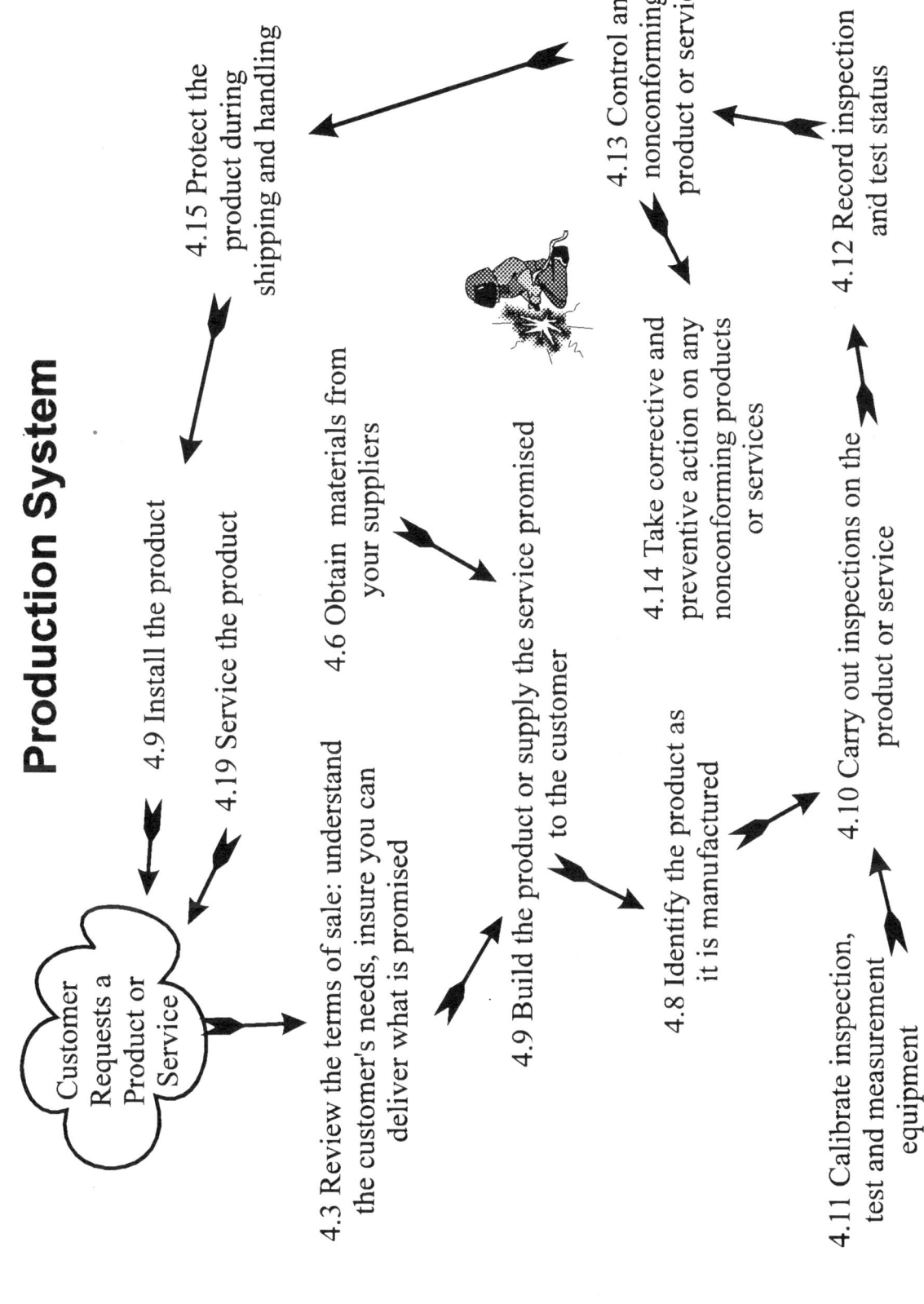

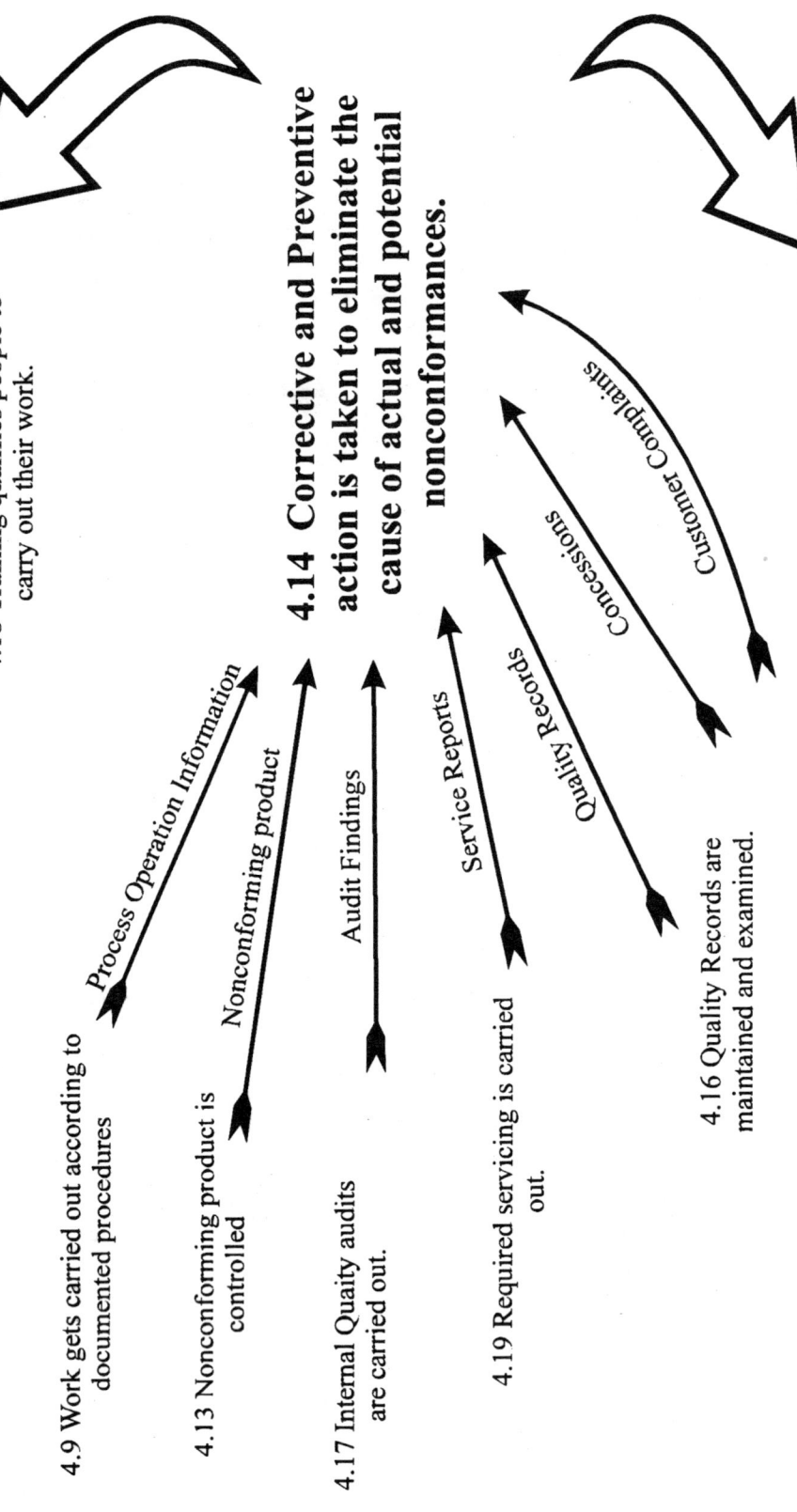

Conformance Calendar

It is difficult to estimate how long it will take for an organization to comply with the Standard and obtain registration. It could take less than six months for a small organization that is using a sound Quality System. It could take as long as three years for a large organization that has a poor Quality System and that is resistant to organizational change. The steps outlined below provide a general template for a compliance plan. Tailor these steps to suit your organization.

1) Establish your intention to seek registration

- Determine the importance of registration in your industry and to your markets.
- Understand the Standard and estimate the effort and schedule for registration.
- Decide between the following alternatives:
    - Seek registration, or
    - Install a Quality System, but delay registration, or
    - Stay as you are for now, reassess the decision later.
- Communicate the decision throughout the top management team.
- Appoint a Management Representative to lead the compliance effort.
- Train the Management Representative to lead the effort. The five-day long "Lead Auditor Training" course, accredited by The Institute of Quality Assurance or the Registration Accreditation Board is recommended.
- Define the scope of the registration sought. Refer to Scope of Registration on page 103. Decide what standard (ISO 9001, ISO 9002 or ISO 9003) to use and what sites to include in the registration effort.
- Communicate the plan to middle management as a minimum, and then throughout the entire organization.
- Establish project management support for the compliance effort.
- Continue to provide top management support for the Management Representative throughout the compliance effort. This is often cited as the single most important factor determining the success of the program.

2) Assess the existing Quality System

- Determine how near the current Quality System is to compliance. Examine all the elements of the Standard across the entire organization. Use the checklist questions from this book as a basis for the assessment.
- Rate each element for each organization as one of the following:
    - Documented system in place and being followed throughout the organization, or
    - Documented system in place, variable compliance across organizations, or
    - Undocumented system in use, or
    - No system in place

3) Design the Quality System

- Appoint compliance leaders to own each element of the Standard. The "Department Responsibilities" table on page 102 will provide a starting point for making these assignments. These element owners need the strong support from the top manager of the identified department. The responsibilities of these element owners include:
    - Learning the requirements of the Standard.
    - Evaluating the existing Quality System for the assigned element. Decide among the following alternatives:
        - The existing system is adequate and will be retained, or
        - The existing system needs several improvements, or
        - The existing system is inadequate or nonexistent.
    - Designing the Quality System that will be used to address the assigned element. For example, a document control system will have to be designed if none now exists. See "Recommended Reading — Design of the Quality System" on page 113.
    - Documenting the Quality System design and reviewing the design with the Management Representative and the other element owners.
- Write the first draft of the quality manual.
- The Management Representative works with these element owners to create a refined compliance plan and schedule.
- Select the accreditation registrar. See "Choosing a Registration Agency" on page 104 for important criteria to consider in this selection.

4) Create Procedures Documents

- Assign people to identify and design the needed processes and write the needed procedure documents and work instructions. See "Hints on Writing Procedure Documents" on page 111.
- Train these procedures writers in the requirements of the Standard, the designing, writing and formatting of procedures, the content of the quality manual and the design of the Quality System created in step 3, above.
- Identify and train the staff who will conduct the internal quality audits.
- Write the final draft of the quality manual.
- Review and approve these procedures documents and work instructions.
- Conduct a "System Audit" to determine if all the requirements of the standard are adequately addressed by the documentation set consisting of the quality manual, procedure documents and work instructions.

5) Implement and Deploy the Quality System

- Communicate the compliance plan to all the workers.
- Deploy the quality manual to all the workers. Train them in use of the quality manual and provide an overview of the Quality System. Emphasize requirements for document control, equipment calibration, retention of quality records, corrective and preventive action, training and any other requirements that may be new to the organization.
- Determine which people need to use which procedure documents.

- Distribute the needed procedure documents.
- Train people to use each procedure that pertains to their work.

6) Conduct Internal Audits

- Create an internal audit plan and schedule. Determine the auditor, schedule and relevant Quality System elements to be audited in each organization.
- Conduct the internal quality audits.
- Take corrective action in each area where the audit has uncovered noncompliances with:
    - The requirements of the Standard,
    - The quality manual, or
    - Documented procedures or work instructions.
- Hold a Management Review.
- Re-audit any area that has systematic noncompliances.
- Revise and reissue any procedure documents that are ineffective.

7) Conduct a Pre-Assessment

- Conduct a pre-assessment by the selected registrar
- Correct the deficiencies identified in the pre-assessment

8) Create a History of Using the Quality System

- The registration auditors will expect to see a history of System usage, substantiated by quality records of approximately six months or more.
- Continue to use the Quality System and to conduct internal audits.
- Continue to take corrective action in each area where the audits uncover noncompliances.

9) Hold the Registration Audit

- Invite the registration agency to conduct a comprehensive audit of the entire organization.
- Celebrate your success with all the people!

10) Monitor and Improve the Quality System

- Continue to conduct internal audits and review and improve the Quality System.
- Host periodic surveillance audits as required by your registration agency.
- Plan your progress towards Total Quality Management.

Department Responsibilities

There are many ways to organize the work of complying with the requirements of ISO 9001. This table suggests one approach to assigning the primary responsibility for leading compliance with each element of the Standard. Adapt this table for use in your own company and industry.

	Top Management	Management Representative	Sales	Engineering	Production	Purchasing	Installation & Service
4.1 Management Responsibility	◆	❖					
4.2 Quality system	❖	◆	❖	❖	❖	❖	❖
4.3 Contract review	❖		◆				◆
4.4 Design control				◆	❖		
4.5 Document and data control	❖	◆	❖	❖	❖	❖	❖
4.6 Purchasing				❖	❖	◆	
4.7 Control of customer-supplied product			❖			◆	
4.8 Product identification and traceability				❖	◆		❖
4.9 Process control					◆		❖
4.10 Inspection and testing					◆		
4.11 Control of inspection, measuring and test equipment		◆		❖	❖	❖	❖
4.12 Inspection and test status					◆		❖
4.13 Control of nonconforming product					◆		❖
4.14 Corrective and preventive action	❖	◆	❖	❖	❖	❖	❖
4.15 Handling, storage, packaging, preservation and delivery				❖	◆		
4.16 Control of quality records		◆	❖	❖	❖	❖	❖
4.17 Internal quality audits	❖	◆	❖	❖	❖	❖	❖
4.18 Training	❖	◆	❖	❖	❖	❖	❖
4.19 Servicing			❖				◆
4.20 Statistical techniques				❖	◆	❖	

Key: ◆ — Lead the effort,   ❖ — Support the effort

Note — Many of the functions assigned to the Management Representative (e.g., training) will be delegated to staff organizations.

Scope of Registration

The extent of your Quality System is defined by the *scope* of your registration. The scope statement will appear on your registration certificate and defines what you can say publicly about the extent of your Quality System. Therefore, deciding on the scope statement is one of the most important decisions to be made in planning your registration effort.

The scope may include one or more geographic locations fully or in part, and may cross or partially include several organizations. To meet the needs of your customers, make the scope statement as inclusive as possible, representing the full extent of your Quality System.

Example Scope Statements

Each of the following are actual scope statements used by companies that are registered to ISO 9001:

"Design and manufacture of die cutting and slitting of pressure sensitive tapes, audio/video tapes, 3.5 inch micro-disk parts, and 5.25 inch floppy disk rings."

"Design and manufacture of high speed robotic mass storage systems."

"Design and manufacture of instrumentation equipment."

"Design and manufacture of marine aids to navigation."

"Design, manufacture and servicing of high end UNIX file servers."

"Design, manufacture, assembly and installation of coil processing equipment for metalworking."

"Design and manufacture of stationary, rotary and reciprocating air compressors."

"Project management, engineering design, procurement of plant and equipment and construction management of process plant projects."

"Engineering, procurement and construction services."

Choosing a Registration Agency

The Registration Accreditation Board (RAB) administers the American National Accreditation Program for Registrars of Quality Systems within the United States. The RAB is affiliated with the American Society for Quality Control and provides accreditation in cooperation with the American National Standards Institute (ANSI). To obtain a list of Quality System Registrars based in the United States and Canada, write to the RAB at 611 E. Wisconsin Ave., PO Box 3005, Milwaukee, WI 53201-3005, USA.

To select a registrar, consider:

- Is the registrar recognized by the customers in the marketplace where you plan to do business? Not all certificates are recognized by an official government agency. Be sure to ask what countries recognize the certificate issued by the registrar.

- What is the source of their accreditation? What is their background and company policy? How long have they been in business? How do they train and qualify their audit teams?

- Does the registrar have experience in your specific industry? How many of the auditors that will visit each site have experience specific to the industry and type of work being audited?

- Is the registrar itself registered to ISO 9000? Will they let you inspect their quality manual?

- Can you talk to other companies they have registered to find out if their clients are satisfied? Do they publish a list of companies that they have registered?

- Is their list of available audit dates consistent with your compliance calendar?

- What will the registrar charge for their services? How are costs for follow-up visits, surveillance audits and cancellations handled? How long will the registration certification last? How will reassessments and surveillance audits be handled? What is their policy regarding suspension, withdrawal or cancellation of their registration?

- Note that the firm you choose to register with cannot for conflict of interest reasons, consult with you. Consider if you would prefer to consult with or register with each candidate firm.

A registration is valid only for a specified length of time, typically three years. Most registrars require that surveillance audits be conducted approximately every 6 months throughout the duration of the registration. Because of this long-term relationship with the registration agency, it is important to choose one that has a philosophy about the Standard that agrees with your company's goals.

The RAB is only one registrar accreditation board. Listed below are several others with their country affiliations:

Danak — Denmark	NACCB — National Association Council for Certification Bodies
DAR — German Accreditation Board	RvC — Dutch Council for Certification
E-Q-NET— European Network for Quality System Assessment and Certification	SAS — Switzerland
FINAS — Finland	SCC — Standards Council of Canada
INMETRO — Brazil	SINCERT— Italy
NA—Norway	SWEDEC— Sweden
NAC-QS — Belgium	TGA — Germany

Related Standards

The following standards are related to ISO 9000. The guidelines are particularly useful because they give prescriptive descriptions of how a company may wish to manage Quality processes to meet the requirements of the contractual standards.

ISO 8402	Quality — Vocabulary
ISO 9000-1	Quality management and quality assurance standards — Guidelines for selection and use. ANSI/ASQC Q9000-1-1994 is the USA Equivalent.
ISO 9000-2	Quality management and quality assurance standards — Part 2: Generic guidelines for application of ISO 9001, ISO 9002 and ISO 9003
ISO 9000-3	Quality management and quality assurance standards — Part 3: Guidelines for the application of ISO 9001 to the development, supply and maintenance of software
ISO 9000-4	Quality management and quality assurance standards — Part 4: Guide to dependability management
ISO 9001	Quality Systems — Model for quality assurance in design/development, production, installation and servicing. ANSI/ASQC Q9001-1994 is the USA equivalent.
ISO 9002	Quality Systems — Model for quality assurance in production, installation and servicing. ANSI/ASQC Q9002-1994 is the USA equivalent.
ISO 9003	Quality Systems — Model for quality assurance in final inspection and test. ANSI/ASQC Q9003-1994 is the USA equivalent.
ISO 9004-1	Quality management and quality system elements — Part 1:Guidelines. ANSI/ASQC Q9004-1-1994 is the USA equivalent.
ISO 9004-2	Quality management and quality system elements — Part 2: Guidelines for services
ISO 9004-3	Quality management and quality system elements — Part 3: Guidelines for processed materials
ISO 9004-4	Quality management and quality system elements — Part 4: Guidelines for quality improvement
ISO 10011-1	Guidelines for auditing quality systems — Part 1: Auditing
ISO 10011-2	Guidelines for auditing quality systems — Part 2: Qualification criteria for quality systems auditors
ISO 10011-3	Guidelines for auditing quality systems — Part 3: Management of audit programs
ISO 10012-1	Quality assurance requirements for measuring equipment — Part 1: Metrological confirmation system for measuring equipment
ISO 10013	Guidelines for developing quality manuals.

ISO/TR 13425 Guidelines for the selection of statistical methods in standardization and specification.

ISO Handbook 3 Statistical methods.

Comparison of ISO 9001 and ISO 9002

The two standards, ISO 9001 and ISO 9002 are very similar. All of the requirements of ISO 9002 are included in ISO 9001. One provision, Design Control, is present in ISO 9001 but absent in ISO 9002. To transform ISO 9001 into ISO 9002 (1994) simply delete paragraph 4.4 (and all its subparagraphs) and change the title to "Quality Systems — Model for quality assurance in production, installation and servicing."

ISO 9001 is appropriate for a company required to design, develop, produce, install, service and supply a product or service. ISO 9002 is appropriate for a company required to produce, install, service and supply a product or service according to an existing design.

The relationship between the paragraph numbers in the two standards is shown in the following table:

ISO 9001 (1994)	ISO 9002 (1987)	ISO 9002 (1994)
4.1 Management responsibility	4.1	4.1
4.2 Quality system	4.2	4.2
4.3 Contract review	4.3	4.3
4.4 Design control	Not Required	N/A
4.5 Document and data control	4.4	4.5
4.6 Purchasing	4.5	4.6
4.7 Control of customer-supplied product	4.6	4.7
4.8 Product identification and traceability	4.7	4.8
4.9 Process control	4.8	4.9
4.10 Inspection and testing	4.9	4.10
4.11 Control of inspection, measuring and test equipment	4.10	4.11
4.12 Inspection and test status	4.11	4.12
4.13 Control of nonconforming product	4.12	4.13
4.14 Corrective and preventive action	4.13	4.14
4.15 Handling, storage, packaging, preservation and delivery	4.14	4.15
4.16 Control of quality records	4.15	4.16
4.17 Internal quality audits	4.16*	4.17
4.18 Training	4.17*	4.18
4.19 Servicing	Not Required	4.19
4.20 Statistical techniques	4.18	4.20

* - Slightly less stringent than ISO 9001.

Changes Made in the 1994 Version of ISO 9001

Directives of the International Organization for Standardization require that all standards be reviewed every five years. The purpose of this review is to ensure that:

- The standards reflect experience gained from its practical application.
- The standards remain stable to facilitate ongoing training and use.
- The standards are usable by companies regardless of size, industry or product offering.

As a result, the ISO 9000 series of standards has been revised and officially adopted in July 1994. The most significant changes from the 1987 version of ISO 9001 are as follows:

- The importance of using third-party registration agencies is now recognized by the language of the Standard.
- The term "customer" replaces the term "purchaser".
- The introduction mentions the assessment of quality capabilities by external parties (i.e., third party registration agencies).
- Subclause 4.1.1, *Quality policy*, includes reference to customers' expectations and needs, and the supplier's internal organizational goals. The quality policy must be defined by "management with executive responsibility".
- Subclause 4.1.2.2, *Resources*, is now broader than "verification resources and personnel" was. It now includes reference to management, trained personnel, work performance, and verification activities. The requirement for independent personnel carrying out design reviews has been removed. The requirement for independence of audit personnel has been moved to 4.17.
- Subclause 4.1.2.3, *Management representative*, must now be appointed by "management with executive responsibility." The Management Representative is now explicitly required to report on the Quality System for the purpose of management review and improvement.
- Subclause 4.2.1, *Quality system-General*, now includes an explicit requirement for a quality manual that defines the documentation structure of the Quality System, including "reference to the quality system procedures and outline [of] the structure of the documentation used in the quality system."
- Subclause 4.2.2, *Quality system procedures*, now clarifies the degree of documentation required for the Quality System. It states that the extent of documented procedures required for work activities shall depend upon "the complexity of the work, the methods used, and the skills and training needed by personnel involved in carrying out the activity."
- Subclause 4.2.3, *Quality planning* is entirely new. It covers Quality System planning and product quality plans. It states that the quality plan for a product, project, or contract may be in the form of a detailed reference to those documented procedures of the Quality System that are appropriate to providing complete assurance of product quality. Most of the information to be considered was in the "Note" in the 1987 version of the Standard.
- Subclause 4.3, *Contract review*, now includes pre-contract tender arrangements as well as contracts and ordering requirements within its scope. It also includes provisions for orders received by verbal means and requires identifying how amendments to a contract will be handled.
- Subclause 4.4, *Design control*, has been expanded to include design validation, and separate requirements for design review and design verification.
- Subclause 4.4.4, *Design input*, must include applicable statutory and regulatory requirements.
- Subclause 4.4.5, *Design output*, specifically states that documents shall be reviewed before release.

- Subclause 4.4.6, *Design Reviews*, is a new section stating that design reviews are mandatory and must be planned, conducted and documented.

- Subclause 4.4.7, *Design Verification*, states that design verification must be carried out at appropriate stages of design and must ensure that "design stage output meets the design stage input requirements."

- Subclause 4.4.8, *Design Validation*, is new and is in addition to "design verification." Design validation must ensure that the product conforms to defined user needs or requirements. This is in addition to design verification which must ensure that design stage output meets design stage input requirements. Design validation follows successful design verification and is normally performed on the final product.

- Subclause 4.4.9, *Design changes*, still requires controls, but no longer requires design control "procedures", since this control naturally falls within the requirement for document and data control.

- Subclause 4.5, *Document and data control*, is expanded to include "data" and "documents of external origin such as standards and customer drawings." The use of electronic media is recognized in a note. Fortunately, "obsolete documents" may be "retained for legal or knowledge-preservation purposes" if they are "suitably identified."

- Subclause 4.6.1, *Purchasing, General*, now requires documented procedures to "ensure that purchased product (see 3.1) conforms to specified requirements."

- Subclause 4.6.4.1, *Supplier verification at subcontractor's premises*, is new. It requires that if source inspection is to be used, it must be specified in the purchasing documents.

- Subclause 4.8, *Product identification and traceability*, requires traceability, where applicable, to begin at receipt rather than during production.

- Subclause 4.9, *Process control*, now includes servicing and has added requirements for maintaining process equipment to ensure continuing process capability. The previous section 4.9.2 on "special processes" has been incorporated into the text of section 4.9. The requirements for qualification of equipment and personnel to carry out process operations shall be specified.

- Subclause 4.10.1, *Inspection and testing, General*, requires the quality plan or documented procedures to specify the required inspection, testing, and quality records.

- Subclause 4.12, *Inspection and test status*, specifies that status "shall be maintained, as defined in the quality plan and/or documented procedures, throughout production, installation and servicing of the product."

- Subclause 4.14, *Corrective and preventive action*, now includes separate requirements for corrective and preventive action. Corrective action refers to eliminating the causes of actual nonconformities, and preventive action refers to eliminating the causes of potential nonconformities. Requirements to implement and record changes in documented procedures and the use of formal procedures for handling customer complaints have been clarified and strengthened.

- Subclause 4.14.3, *Preventive action*, now requires that "relevant information on actions taken is submitted for management review."

- Subclause 4.16, *Control of quality records*, allows for storage on electronic or other media. Procedures must address access to quality records. Records no longer have to be "identifiable to the product involved."

- Subclause 4.18, *Training*, now requires documented procedures.

- Subclause 4.20 *Statistical techniques*, requires statistical techniques to be identified.

The Concept of a Process

The concept that all work is accomplished by a process is at the foundation of the ISO 9000 family of standards. A process has inputs, adds value to those inputs and produces outputs as illustrated below.

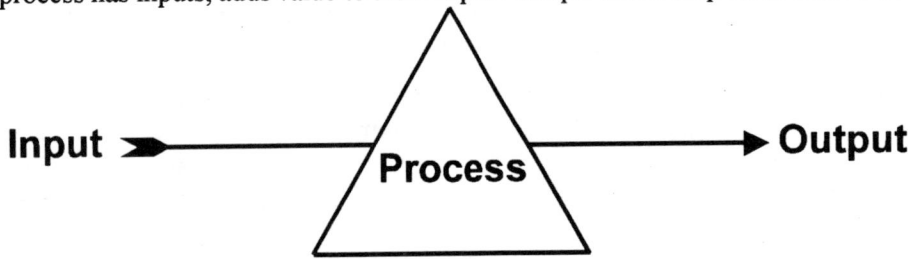

	Input	Process	Output
Description	Materials, information or sub-assemblies provided by others and required to carry out the process	An activity that transforms the inputs into the outputs	Materials, information, product or services provided to others
Characteristics	- Provided by others - Tangible or intangible - Raw materials, assemblies or an intermediate product - Often the output of a previous process.	- Adds value to input - Transforms inputs to outputs - Involves people and resources.	- Provided to others - Tangible or intangible - Provides value to the end customer, or - Creates a useful or necessary intermediate process
Examples	Chopped meat, bun Blank form, billing information Requirements Plastic, rubber Crude oil Endorsed check Solder, wires	Cook lunch Create invoice Write software Manufacture syringe Refine oil Cash check Soldering	Hamburger Invoice Computer software Syringe Gasoline Cash, updated account Completed cable assembly

Often processes are connected end to end to create a network of processes. This "supply chain" includes product related flows from left to right, and information flows between the supplier's process, your process and the customer's process as shown below:

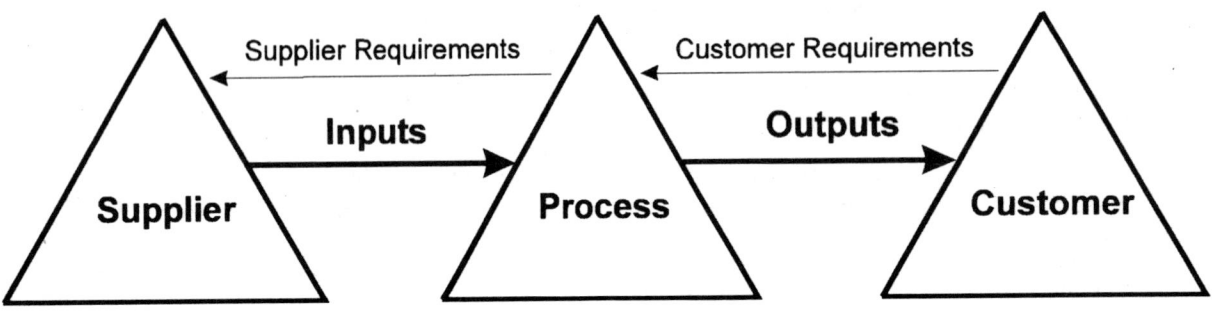

This is often referred to as the *customer - supplier model*.

Hints on Writing Procedures Documents

Much of the Quality System is made up of documented procedures. Your registration efforts, and the effectiveness of your Quality System will depend heavily on well-written procedures documents. The following guidelines may be helpful:

- Create a simple design for each element of the Quality System before writing procedure documents.

- Understand the requirements of the Standard before proceeding. It may be useful to take each "checklist" question from this book and turn it into a positive statement to provide guidance on how to proceed. For example, the checklist for Section 4.15.6 asks "Does a list of approved carriers exist?" Turn this around to state: "Create a list of approved carriers." If this is pertinent to your business, be sure to include it in the procedures document.

- Seek guidance from several sources. These may include the ISO 9004-1 Standard, experts on the process from within your company, experts from other registered companies, books or other literature on particular processes (see "Recommended Reading" on page 113).

- Use existing documentation as much as possible, especially if it is clearly written and understood by the users. Avoid writing how you *wish* the process were carried out. Describe how it actually *is* carried out.

- Establish a style guide for writing procedure documents. Select authors who are skilled at technical writing and who are familiar with the process being described. Provide authors with examples of good (and notoriously bad) procedures documents and writing style. Train the document authors in the requirements of the Standard, the concept of a process and your requirements for procedure document content, format, approval and document control.

- Consider using professional technical writers to assist in the documentation effort.

- Define the boundaries of the process. Determine and write down precisely the purpose of the process, where it begins and where it ends. Identify what events trigger the process (i.e., what causes the process to be carried out) and what is the output or result of the process.

- Flowchart the process before trying to describe it. Flowcharting can be done most easily by gathering a group of process experts (the people who perform the process) and having them write each process activity, work product or required input materials or information on individual self-stick notes. Arrange these notes in a time order sequence on an easel that can been seen by the entire group. Add and delete steps, work products and inputs until the flow is complete and at a level of detail consistent with the skill of the workers and the complexity of the task.

- Check the flowchart for accuracy and completeness. Insure all the inputs and outputs are included and connected to activities. Include all the decisions that are made and connect the paths of both the "yes" and "no" branches of each decision. Determine and document what happens in exception cases such as a tool breaking, an input missing or an error being detected. Talk through each step from start to finish and have the group verify accuracy.

- Determine who carries out each task and makes each decision on the flowchart. Determine the source of each input and the destination of each output.

- Simplify the flowchart if it contains unnecessary steps or excessive detail.

- Write in a clear, simple, imperative style. State only what actions need to be carried out, what decisions need to be made, the basis for each decision, who has the authority and responsibility to make each decision and to carry out each action. Avoid gratuitous advice and the word "should". Eliminate subjective words such as: "as appropriate", "as needed", "immediately, "may", "often", and "sometimes". Clearly separate mandatory steps from suggestions. Key the text to the flowchart steps.

- Write, using a style and level of detail that is consistent with the experience, training, skill and educational level of the intended process operators (i.e., document users). Have intended users read and comment on the document before it is issued.

- Use diagrams, charts, drawings, forms and representative examples liberally to make the documentation as clear and easy to use as possible.

- Include definitions of terms and acronyms used in the process. Be sure that the same term is not given different definitions by related process documents. Include templates, outlines or representative examples of documents or other outputs of the process.

- Reference related procedures documents, work instructions and standards documents. Ensure that each procedures document is referenced by the quality manual.

- Identify quality records and their retention requirements to ensure compliance with Section 4.16 of the Standard.

- Make clear who has responsibility and authority to carry out each process step and approve documents and actions.

- Include a document title, document number, issue date, revision level, revision history, author name and title, approval authority and authorizing signature.

- As detail is added to the procedures, be certain it is accurate.

- Have your internal quality auditors read the procedures to determine if they comply with the Standard and are sufficiently clear and specific to establish the basis for an audit.

- Train users on the operation of the process and the content of the procedure documents before they are issued. Incorporate suggestions made by users during these training sessions into the final documents.

- Prepare the author to accept and incorporate suggestions for improving the document. These suggestions may come from users or from the formal corrective and preventive action system. Design a document control system that helps to rapidly incorporate improvements into the documents, gains the necessary approvals, trains users on the changes and deploys the revised procedures to all users.

Recommended Reading — Design of the Quality System

Below are listed books that can provide useful guidance in designing elements of your Quality System. They present information far beyond what is required for compliance with the Standard and represent excellent references useful in creating or improving your Quality System. They are listed according to the section of the Standard they are most relevant to.

4.1 - Management Responsibility
Juran on Leadership for Quality, J. M. Juran, 1989, ISBN 0-02-916682-9.

4.2 Quality System
Juran's Quality Control Handbook, Fourth Edition, J. M. Juran, Frank M. Gryna, 1988, ISBN 0-07-033176-6.

4.4 Design Control
Product Development: Success Through Product And Cycle-Time Excellence, Michael E. McGrath, Michael T. Anthony, Amran R. Shapiro. ISBN 0-7506-9289-8.
Revolutionizing Product Development: Quantum Leaps In Speed, Efficiency, And Quality, Steven C. Wheelright, Kim B. Clark. ISBN 0-02-905515-6.
Developing Products In Half The Time, Preston G. Smith and Donald G. Reinertsen. ISBN 0-442-00243-2.
Total Quality Development: A Step-By-Step Guide To World-Class Concurrent Engineering, Don Clausing, 1994, ISBN 0-7918-0035-0.
Managing The Development Of New Products, Milton D. Rosenau, Jr., John J. Moran. ISBN 0-442-01395-7.
Faster New Product Development: Getting The Right Product To Market Quickly. M. D. Rosenau, 1990, ISBN 0-8144-5942-0.

4.6 Purchasing
Buying and Supplying Quality, Richard Weber, Ross Johnson, 1993, ISBN 0-87389-253-4.

4.9 Process Control
Process Quality Management & Improvement Guidelines, Roger B. Ackerman, Roberta J. Coleman, Elias Leger, John C. MacDorman, 1989, order from AT&T Customer Information Center, Phone 1-800-432-6600, Select Code No. 500-049.

4.10 Inspection and Testing
Inspection and Inspection Management, Charles Suntag, 1993, ISBN 0-87389-174-0.

4.11 Control of Inspection, Measuring and Test Equipment
Measurement and Calibration for Quality Assurance, Alan S. Morris, 1991, ISBN 0-13-567652-5.

4.13 Control of Nonconforming Product
MRB (Materials Review Board) Engineering Handbook, Robert C. Noe, 1993, ISBN 0-87389-199-6.

4.14 Corrective and Preventive Action
Root Cause Analysis: A Tool for Total Quality Management, Paul F. Wilson, Larry D. Dell, and Gaylord F. Anderson, 1993, ISBN 0-87389-163-5.

4.17 Internal Quality Audits
The Quality Audit: A Management Evaluation Tool, Charles A. Mills, 1989, ISBN 0-07-042428-4.

4.20 Statistical Techniques
Quantitative Methods for Quality and Productivity Improvement, Marilyn K. Hart, Robert F. Hart, 1989, ISBN 0-87389-056-6.

Total Quality Management

ISO 9001 presents a basic model for Quality Assurance. Within the United States, the Malcolm Baldrige National Quality Award (MBNQA) presents a model for ultimate excellence. The purpose of this section is to help the reader understand the ways in which the requirements of a Total Quality Management (TQM) system go beyond requirements of the ISO 9001 Standard. This understanding can help to make ISO 9001 compliance a solid foundation for TQM.

Core values and concepts upon which the MBNQA is built are described below as an example of a Total Quality Management system. The requirements of ISO 9001 relevant to each principle are described on the right. In short, ISO 9001 is an excellent foundation and starting point for creating a Total Quality Management system. It lacks specific requirements in the area of cycle time reduction, efficiency, elimination of rework, direct measurement of customer satisfaction and employee well-being, and several other elements of a Total Quality Management system.

Total Quality Management Principles

Customer-Driven Quality

Quality is judged by the customer. This concept includes not only product and service attributes that meet basic customer requirements, but also includes those that enhance them and differentiate them from competing offerings. Customer-driven quality is directed toward keeping customers and gaining market share. It demands awareness of developments in technology, and rapid and flexible response to customer and market requirements. This extends beyond reducing defects and errors, meeting specifications and reducing complaints.

ISO 9001

Contract Review

The customer contract is understood and complied with. Work is carried out using controlled processes, and verified to ensure it meets specifications. Defects, errors, and customer complaints are investigated, and corrective and preventive actin are taken.

Leadership

A company's senior leaders must create a customer orientation, clear and visible quality values, and high expectations. Substantial personal commitment and involvement is required to reinforce quality values and expectations. These values extend to include public responsibility and corporate citizenship. The senior leaders must commit to the growth and development of the entire workforce and should encourage participation and creativity by all people. Senior leaders serve as role models reinforcing the values and encouraging leadership in all levels of management.

Management Responsibility

Management responsibility requires the deployment of a quality policy, clarification of organizational roles and responsibilities, providing adequate verification resources and personnel and appointing a management representative. The Quality System is also reviewed by management to ensure its effectiveness.

Continuous Improvement

Processes must be improved continuously to achieve the highest levels of quality and competitiveness. These improvements may be of several types: 1) enhancing value to customers through new and improved products and services; 2) reducing errors, defects, and waste; 3) improving responsiveness and cycle time performance; 4) improving productivity and effectiveness in the use of all resources; and 5) improving the company's performance and leadership position in fulfilling its public responsibilities and serving as a role model for corporate citizenship. Improvement is driven not only by the objective to provide better product and service quality, but also by the need to be responsive and efficient.

Corrective and Preventive Action

Nonconforming products and services are identified and the cause of the defect is identified and investigated. Processes, work operations and customer complaints are analyzed to detect and eliminate potential causes of defects.

Management review of the Quality System ensures its continued suitability and effectiveness.

Employee Participation and Development

Increasingly, a company's ability to meet its quality and performance objectives depends on work force quality and involvement. This close link between employee satisfaction and customer satisfaction makes measuring and improving employee satisfaction an important part of TQM. Companies need to invest in the development of the work force and to seek new avenues to involve employees in problem solving and decision making. Factors that bear on the safety, health, well-being and morale of employees need to be part of the company's continuous objectives.

Training

Training requirements for all those whose work affects product or service quality are identified. Workers are adequately trained before being assigned to carry out their tasks.

In addition, the responsibility and authority of many personnel are made clear.

Fast Response

Success in competitive markets increasingly demands ever-shorter cycles for new or improved product and service introductions. Faster and more flexible response to customers is now a more critical requirement of business management. Major improvements in response time often require work organizations, work processes and work paths to be simplified and shortened. To accomplish such improvement, attention must be given to measuring cycle time performance, making response time a key indicator of work unit improvements.

Conformance to Specifications

Fast response is not specifically addressed by the standard. Time commitments established by the contract, design input requirements and purchasing requirements must be met.

Design Quality and Prevention

In general, costs of preventing problems at the design stage are much lower than costs of correcting problems which occur later in the process. Design quality includes the creation of fault-tolerant (robust) processes and products.

The design-to-introduction ("product generation") cycle time must be continuously reduced by improving all product generation processes.

Long-Range Outlook

Achieving quality and market leadership requires a company to have a strong future orientation to customer, employees, suppliers, stockholders, and the community. A major part of the long-term commitment relates to the development of employees and suppliers, and to fulfilling public responsibilities and serving as a corporate citizenship role model.

Management by Fact

Pursuit of quality and operational performance goals of the company requires that process management be based upon reliable information, data, and analysis. Facts, data, and analysis support a variety of company purposes, such as planning, reviewing company performance, improving operations, and comparing company quality performance with benchmarks. A system of performance indicators, measuring characteristics of products, services, processes, and operations, tied to customer and company performance requirements represents a clear and objective basis for aligning all activities of the company towards common goals.

Partnership Development

Companies can often accelerate achievement of their overall goals by building internal and external partnerships. Internal partnerships might include labor-management cooperation, employee development, cross-training or new work organizations. External partnerships might include those with customers, suppliers, and education organizations. Strategic partnerships or alliances might offer a company entry into new markets or provide a basis for new products or services.

Design Control

Design control requirements of the standard include documented design procedures, planning, documented design input, design output and design reviews, design verification and validation and control of design changes.

Corrective and preventive action moves problem detection forward in the design cycle.

Quality System

The organization structure, defined processes, trained staff and verification resources establishes an organization prepared to do business in the long term.

Assessment of suppliers helps in the development of reliable suppliers able to carry out long-term relationships.

Quality Records, Audits

Quality records are maintained to demonstrate achievement of the required quality and effective operation of the Quality System. Where statistical techniques are used to verify process capability and product characteristics, these techniques must be valid. A system of internal quality audits determines if quality activities comply with planned arrangements. Management reviews examine data describing the effectiveness of the Quality System.

Assessment of Subcontractors

Assessment of suppliers helps in the development of suppliers able to work as reliable partners. Coordinating contract review activities with the customer helps to build a customer partnership.

Corporate Responsibility and Citizenship

Corporate responsibility refers to basic expectations of the company — business ethics, and protection of public health, public safety, and the environment. Inclusion of public responsibility areas within a Quality System means not only meeting all local, state, and federal legal and regulatory requirements, but also treating these and related requirements as areas for continuous improvement beyond mere compliance.

Process Control

Process control requires that work be carried out in a suitable working environment. This includes meeting all local, state and national legal and regulatory requirements.

Bibliography

In addition to several of the standards listed on page 105, the following references were used to prepare this book:

ANSI / ASQC Q90 ISO 9001 Guidelines, for use by the Chemical and Process Industries, ASQC Chemical and Process Industries Division, Chemical Interest Committee, 1992, ASQC Quality Press, ISBN 0-87389-196-1.

ISO 9000: Preparing for Registration, James L. Lamprecht, 1992, ASQC Quality Press, ISBN 0-8247-8741-2.

A Guidebook to ISO 9000 and ANSI/ASQC Q90, Ronald J. Cottman, 1993, ASQC Quality Press, ISBN 0-87389-194-5.

ISO 9000: Handbook of Quality Standards and Compliance, Bureau of Business Practice, 1992, ISBN 0-87622-186-X.

ISO 9000 International Standards for Quality Management, International Organization for Standardization, 1991, ISBN 92-67-10165-X.

Malcolm Baldrige National Quality Award, Award Criteria, 1993, United States Department of Commerce.

The Role of ISO 9000 Standards in Continuous Improvement, April Cormaci and Ian Durand, Quality Systems Update, October, 1993.

Sticking With Flowcharts, Leland R. Beaumont, Quality Progress, July, 1993.

Updating the ISO 9000 Quality Standards: Responding to Marketplace Needs, Ian G. Durand, Donald W. Marquardt, Robert W. Peach, and James C. Pyle, Quality Progress, July, 1993.

The ISO 9000 Handbook, Second Edition, Edited by Robert W. Peach, 1994, CEEM Information Services.

Glossary and Index

Many terms used in the Standard either have specialized meanings or are unfamiliar to people newly involved with Quality Systems and standards. This glossary clarifies the terms used in this book or provides the definition of the term from the ISO 9000 family, if it is available. Terms defined in this glossary are indicated by use of *italics*. To provide an index, the page number where the topic is discussed in the text appears immediately after selected terms.

Accreditation Procedure by which an authoritative body gives formal recognition that a body or person is competent to carry out specific tasks.

ANSI 104, American National Standards Institute. The agency that represents the USA in the International Organization for Standardization (ISO). They can be contacted at 11 West 42nd Street, 13th floor, New York, NY 10036, USA (Telephone 212-642-4900).

ASQC The American Society for Quality Control. An organization of professionals dedicated to the advancement of quality through leadership and action. They can be contacted at: 310 West Wisconsin Avenue, Milwaukee, WI 53203, USA.

Audit A planned, independent and documented assessment to determine whether agreed-upon requirements are being met. See *Quality Audit*.

Auditor A person who is qualified to carry out a *Quality Audit*.

Calibration 61, Adjusting a measuring instrument to make it accurate. The set of operations which establish, under specified conditions, the relationship between values indicated by a measuring instrument or measuring system and the corresponding values of a quantity realized by a reference standard.

Chief Executive Top ranking manager of the organization.

Certification Procedure by which a third party gives written assurance that a product, process or service conforms to specific requirements.

Certification Audit Synonymous with *registration audit*.

Compliance An affirmative indication or judgment that the supplier of a product or service has met the requirements of the relevant specifications, contract or regulation; also the state of meeting the requirements.

Conformance An affirmative indication or judgment that a product or service has met the requirements of the relevant specifications, contract or regulations; also the state of meeting the requirements.

Concession 69, Use of known bad materials or sale of known bad product or a rebate given in return for accepting bad product. Written authorization to use or release a quantity of material, components or stores already produced but which do not conform to the specified requirements.

Contract 12, Agreed requirements between a supplier and customer transmitted by any means.

Controlled Orderly, repeatable, manageable, predictable.

Corrective Action 73, Action taken to eliminate the causes of an existing nonconformance, defect or other undesirable situation in order to prevent recurrence.

Customer Recipient of a product provided by the supplier. Notes: 1) In a contractual situation, the customer is called the "purchaser". 2) The customer may be, for example, the ultimate consumer, user, beneficiary or purchaser. 3) The customer can be either external or internal to the organization.

Defect The nonfulfilment of intended use requirements.

Design Input 30, Design objectives, typically provided in the form of product performance *specifications*, product descriptions with specifications relating to configuration, composition, incorporated elements and other design features.

Design Output 31, The end result of the design activity, such as drawings, *specifications*, instructions, computer programs or other software or servicing procedures.

Design Review 31, A formal, documented, comprehensive and systematic examination of a design to evaluate the design requirements and the capability of the design to meet these requirements and to identify problems and propose solutions.

Findings A conclusion of importance based on observations.

F.O.B. Abbreviation for "Free on Board", meaning without charge to the customer for delivery on board or into a carrier at a specified point or location.

Gantt Chart 29, A bar chart that depicts project progress or planned tasks in relation to time. It is often used in planning or tracking a project.

Grade A category or rank given to entities, having the same functional use but different requirements for quality.

Hardware 11, Tangible, discrete product with distinctive form. Note: Hardware normally consists of manufactured, constructed or fabricated pieces, parts and/or assemblies.

IEC 7, International Electrotechnical Commission. A worldwide organization that produces standards in the electrical and electronic fields.

Inspection 55, Activities such as measuring, examining, testing or gauging one or more characteristics of a product or service and comparing these with specified requirements to determine conformity.

International Organization for Standardization (ISO), The specialized international agency for standardization, at present comprising the national standards bodies of 91 countries. The American National Standards Institute (*ANSI*) is the member body representing the United States. The address of ISO is: ISO, Case Postale 56, CH-1211 Geneva 20, Switzerland.

ISO The *International Organization for Standardization*.

ISO 9000 Family All those international Standards produced by Technical Committee ISO/TC 176. Notes: At present, the family comprises a) all the international Standards numbered ISO 9000 through ISO 9004, including all parts of ISO 9000 and ISO 9004; b) all the international Standards numbered ISO 10001 through 10020, including all parts; and c) ISO 8402.

— The Standard Interpretation

Job-shop 22, A service that provides made-to-order products using general purpose equipment. Each job is unique, having few similarities to the next job.

Management Representative 17, The person with the defined authority and responsibility to carry out the requirements of ISO 9001.

MBNQA 114, Malcolm Baldrige National Quality Award. Awards are made annually to recognize US companies that excel in quality management and quality achievement. For more information, write to: Malcolm Baldrige National Quality Award, National Institute of Standards and Technology, Route 270 and Quince Orchard Road, Administration Building, Room A537, Gaithersburg, MD 20899, USA.

NIST 62, National Institute of Standards and Technology. An agency of the United States Department of Commerce, the institute develops measurement standards and techniques for American science and industry and for other government agencies. NIST also helps U.S. companies adopt new technologies to increase their international competitiveness.

Noncompliance A deviation from the requirements of the Standard.

Nonconformity 68, The nonfulfilment of specified requirements.

Objective Evidence 85, Qualitative or quantitative information, records or statements of fact pertaining to the quality of an item or service or to the existence and implementation of a *Quality System* element, which is based on observation, measurement or test and which can be verified.

Organization Company, corporation, firm, enterprise or institution, or part thereof, whether incorporated or not, public or private, that has its own functions and administration.

Preventive Action 73, Action taken to eliminate the causes of a potential nonconformance, defect or other undesirable situation in order to prevent occurrence.

Procedure A specified way to perform an activity. See *Procedures Manual*.

Procedures Manual 22, A written description of what operations are to be performed to carry out a particular *process*. See "Hints on Writing Procedures Documents" on page 111.

Process Set of interrelated resources and activities which transforms inputs into outputs. Notes: Resources may include personnel, finance, facilities, equipment, techniques and methods. See "the concept of a process" on page 110.

Process Control 51, A system of measurements, decisions and adjustments within a *process* intended to ensure the output of the *process* conforms with pertinent *specifications*.

Processed Materials 11, Tangible product generated by transforming raw material into a desired state. Notes: 1) The state of processed material can be liquid, gas, particulate material, ingot, filament or sheet. 2) Processed material is typically delivered in drums, bags, tanks, cylinders, cans, pipelines or rolls. Characteristics: By their nature, processed (bulk) materials present unique difficulties with regard to the verification of the product at important points in the production process. This increases the importance of the use of statistical sampling and evaluation procedures and their application to in-process controls and final product specifications. See ISO 9004-3.

Product 11, Result of activities or *processes*. See notes 2,3 and 4 in section 3.1 of the Standard.

Purchaser The customer in a contractual situation.

Qualified 17, Verified as capable of providing the required performance.

Quality Totality of characteristics of an entity that bear on its ability to satisfy stated and implied needs.

Quality Assurance All the planned and systematic activities implemented within the Quality System, and demonstrated as needed, to provide adequate confidence that an entity will fulfill requirements for quality. Notes: 1) There are both internal and external purposes for quality assurance: a) internal quality assurance: within an organization, quality assurance provides confidence to the management; b) external quality assurance: in contractual or other situations, quality assurance provides confidence to the customers or others. 2) Some quality control and quality assurance actions are interrelated. 3) Unless requirements for quality fully reflect the needs of the user, quality assurance may not provide adequate confidence.

Quality Audit 85, A systematic and independent examination to determine whether *quality* activities and related results comply with planned arrangements. The audit also determines whether these arrangements are implemented effectively and are suitable to achieve objectives.

Quality Control Operational techniques and activities used to fulfill requirements for quality. Notes: 1) Quality control involves operational techniques and activities aimed both at monitoring a process and at eliminating causes of unsatisfactory performance at all stages of the quality loop in order to achieve economic effectiveness. 2) Some quality control and quality assurance actions are interrelated.

Quality Improvement Actions taken throughout the organization to increase the effectiveness and efficiency of activities and processes in order to provide added benefits to both the organization and its customers.

Quality Management All activities of the overall management function that determine the *quality policy*, objectives and responsibilities, and implement them by means such as quality planning, quality control, quality assurance and quality improvement within the Quality System. Notes: 1) Quality management is the responsibility of all levels of management but must be led by top management. Its implementation involves all members of the organization. 2) In quality management, consideration is given to economic aspects.

Quality Manual 22, A document stating the quality policy and describing the Quality System of an organization. See section 4.2.

Quality Plan A document setting out the specific quality practices, resources and sequence of activities relevant to a particular product, service, contract or project.

Quality Policy 15, Overall intentions and direction of an organization with regard to *quality*, as formally expressed by top management. Note: The quality policy forms one element of the corporate policy and is authorized by top management. See section 4.1.1.

Quality Records 81, Written records that are retained in accordance with the requirements of Section 4.16 of ISO 9001.

Quality System 21, Organizational structure, procedures, processes and resources needed to implement *quality management*. Notes: 1) The Quality System should be as comprehensive as needed to meet the quality objectives. 2) The Quality System of an organization is designed primarily to meet the internal managerial needs of the organization. It is broader than the requirements of a particular customer, who evaluates only the relevant part of the Quality System. 3) For contractual or mandatory quality assessment purposes, demonstration of the implementation of the identified Quality System elements may be required. See section 4.2

Quality System Audit 85, A documented activity to verify, by examination and evaluation of objective evidence, that applicable elements of the Quality System are suitable and have been developed, documented and effectively implemented in accordance with specified requirements. See Section 4.17.

RAB 104, Registration Accreditation Board administers the American National Accreditation Program for Registrars of Quality Systems.

Registration Procedure by which a body indicates relevant characteristics of a product, process or service, or particulars of a body or person, and then includes or registers the product, process or service in an appropriate publicly available list.

Registration Agency An organization, accredited by a registration board, authorized to provide certification or registration of client companies.

Registration Audit A comprehensive *quality audit*, conducted by a *registration agency*, for the purposes of establishing *registration* of an organization. Synonymous with *Certification Audit*

Responsibility Being obliged to answer — as for one's actions — to an authority that may impose a penalty for failure.

Root Cause A fundamental deficiency that results in a nonconformance and must be corrected to prevent recurrence of the same or similar nonconformance.

Service 11, Result generated by activities at the interface between the suppler and the customer and by supplier internal activities to meet the customer needs. Notes: 1) The supplier or the customer may be represented at the interface by personnel or equipment. 2) Customer activities at the interface with the supplier may be essential to the service delivery. 3) Delivery or use of tangible product may form part of the service delivery. 4) A service may be linked with the manufacture and supply of tangible product.
  Characteristics: The characteristics of a service can differ from those of other products and can include such aspects as personnel, waiting time, delivery time, hygiene, credibility and communication delivered directly to the final customer. Customer assessment, often very subjective, is the ultimate measure of the quality of a service. See ISO 9004-2.

Servicing 91, product support taking place after the initial delivery of the product.

Software 11, An intellectual creation consisting of information expressed through supporting medium. Notes: 1) Software can be in the form of concepts, transactions or procedures. 2) A computer program is a specific example of software.
  Characteristics: The process of development, supply and maintenance of software is different from that of most other types of industrial products in that there is no distinct manufacturing phase. Software does not "wear out" and, consequently, quality activities during the design phase are of paramount importance to the final quality of the product. See ISO 9000-3 for additional guidance.

Special Processes 52, Processes used in the production of products whose quality cannot be fully verified later by nondestructive inspection of the product. Examples include welding, soldering, heat treating or plating metal, forming plastic, baking foods, writing software or writing a legal document.

Specifications Documents that prescribe requirements with which the product or service has to conform. Note: A specification would refer to or include drawings, patterns or other relevant documents and should also indicate the means and the criteria whereby conformity can be checked.

Standard An acknowledged measure of comparison for quantitative or qualitative value; a criterion, especially ISO 9001 or a related Standard.

Subcontractor An organization that provides a product to the supplier.

Supplier Organization that provides a product to the customer. Notes: 1) In a contractual situation, the supplier may be called the "contractor". 2) The supplier may be, for example, the producer, distributor, importer, assembler or service organization. 3) The supplier can be either external or internal to the organization.

System A group of interacting, interrelated, or interdependent elements forming a complex whole. An organized set of interrelated ideas or principles. See *Quality System*.

Tender 12, Offer made by a supplier in response to an invitation to satisfy a contract award to provide product.

Testing A means of determining an item's capability to meet specified requirements by subjecting them to a set of physical, chemical, environmental, or operating actions and conditions.

TickIT Means of registering software systems based on the ISO 9000-3 standard. The scheme was developed jointly by the United Kingdom Department of Trade and Industry (DTI) and the British Computer Society.

TQM 114, Total Quality Management. A management structure where the goal of every employee is to achieve ever increasing levels of customer satisfaction. The Malcolm Baldrige National Quality Award criteria are often used to provide a working definition of TQM.

Traceability 49, The ability to trace the history, application or location of an item or activity by means of recorded identification.

Validation 33, The process of evaluating software to ensure compliance with specified requirements.

Verification 32, Reviewing, inspecting, testing, checking, auditing, or otherwise establishing and documenting whether items, processes, services, or documents conform to specified requirements.

Waiver See *concession*

Work Instructions 23, A written description of how to carry out the operations of a particular process.

— The Standard Interpretation

CORRECTIVE ACTION REQUEST:

Date:_____ Facility/Location _____ Department:_____

Observation: Number:_____   Response Due Date:_____

Subject:_____

Standard / Document Reference:_____
Description:
_____
_____
_____
_____
_____
_____

Signed: _____

Response: Assigned to:_____

Root Cause:
_____
_____
_____
_____

Corrective Action Taken: Due Date:_____
_____
_____
_____
_____

Preventive Action Taken: Due Date:_____
_____
_____
_____
_____

Signed: _____ Date:_____

Permission to copy this page freely is granted by ISO Easy, PO Box 21, Middletown, NJ 07748

Summary and Structure of the ISO 9001 Standard

4.1 Management Responsibility
Executive management actively supports achievement of product and service quality.

4.2 Quality System
The organization structure, staff, procedures, and other resources needed to manage quality are in place.

4.3 Contract Review	4.4 Design Control	4.6 Purchasing	4.7 Control of Customer Supplied Product	4.8 Product Identification and Traceability	4.10 Inspection and Testing	4.12 Inspection and Test Status	4.13 Control of Nonconforming Product	4.15 Handling, Storage, Packaging, Preservation and Delivery	4.19 Servicing
You and your customers understand and agree what will be provided.	The innovative design process is orderly, repeatable and ensures that design output meets design input requirements.	Your Quality System extends to include selection and management of your suppliers.	Sub-assemblies provided by your customer are cared for.	The specification for each component can be identified throughout its life.	Product is inspected as it is received, during construction and when completed.	Test and inspection results are recorded.	Bad product is identified to avoid accidental use.	Products are protected and preserved during handling, storage, packaging and shipping.	Customer support is provided as promised.

4.9 Process Control
Process steps that affect product and service quality are effectively managed.

4.14 Corrective and Preventive Action
When problems occur, the processes are analyzed and fixed.

4.5 Document and Data Control	4.16 Control of Quality Records	4.17 Internal Quality Audits	4.11 Control of Inspection, Measuring and Test Equipment	4.20 Statistical Techniques
Procedure and project documents are authoritative, current and available.	Records generated as the Quality System is used are available.	Independent staff verify that activities are carried out consistent with the Quality System.	Test and measurement equipment is calibrated.	Statistical techniques used for controlling processes are valid.

4.18 Training
People are qualified to perform their work.